Aaron,

It was n
you. I pray &
of glory in your life. I see God
breathing on every dream and vision
that he has given you. Your house
shall prosper and flourish in this
next season, for the lord is making
more space for your voice.

THE K-GENE

PRINCIPLES FOR ATTAINING YOUR DESTINY

BREON N. WELLS

Apostle Breon N Wells
(2017)

THE K-GENE 2

INTRODUCTION

Did you know that you are genetically predisposed to win? Victory doesn't have to be an elusive concept, but can be a sure reality for the believer. Unfortunately, most people don't know nor profess this truth. From your very creation, every fiber of your being was infused with the DNA of an overcomer, and peace and prosperity have always been your inheritance. If these last few sentences have made you feel valued and enriched then I am glad, yet they should also make you feel cautious. These sentences represent your potential, not a guaranteed outcome. You see, the grave is full of people with potential and vision. Many benefactors of inheritances lie in cold graves never having been reconciled with their rightful possessions and livelihood. Even among the living there are people who fall short of their full potential and never answer the deepest question within: "Who am I?" Inheritances, like trusteeships, are for specific set times and qualifications, meaning that access to such allotments is based on proper alignment with the right system. The conditions of these terms and the rules of the proper system are set forth by the one who originally bequeaths the inheritance.

It is a sad fact, but many people in the body of Christ are bereft of a proper understanding of their identity. Ask most Christians who they are, and they will rattle off a list of characteristics or skill sets instead of an actual identity. There are even Christian leaders who passionately toil in ministry, yet lack an understanding of who they are. We've mistakenly assumed that our gifts are our identities. This explains why insecurity abounds, and why people often suffer from identity crises when they run into someone who may be better at displaying the same gifted qualities that they do. The result of this confusion and ignorance is that competition among believers is common in churches, ushering in divisive spirits where unity is essential. Furthermore, these competitive people gather in a church setting and become frustrated and unhappy, because they do not understand their purpose. This leads such people to blame church as the cause of all of their spiritual, financial, and social woes. I believe that this frustration with church comes from a cultural misunderstanding of the institution and its original intent. Could it be that this lack of proper understanding has led us to place undue expectations on a system that was meant for a totally different purpose? Perhaps we feel unfulfilled because we have been seeking our identity in a structure that was only meant to complement the preordained identity that God entrusted to each man from the beginning.

I believe that while some are turned away from Christianity because of their frustration with church, others are compelled to pursue The Truth further, despite their discontentment. This pursuit has given birth to a generation that defines their identity in Kingdom ideology rather than church functions. This pursuit is both healthy and necessary. If we never solve the riddle of who we are, we'll end up missing out on the divinely assured inheritance that was set aside specifically for us! If you never wrestle down your identity, that failure will forever affect your ability to operate and command things that are necessary for you to function in this Christian walk. Failing to secure your individual purpose in God will cause an incomplete imagery of the body of Christ, resulting in a strain on us all.

Although God could very well disclose your identity and purpose to others, it is not theirs to reveal to you. If this were to happen, they would be the one who called you, and thus your success or failure would lie in their hands. God is too wise, and loves you too much to put your future in the hands of another human. You will only find your purpose as you seek out God, the author and finisher of your faith, and the one who placed His genetic capability within you.

This gene is called "the Kingdom Gene" and learning how to activate it will be essential to you receiving the inheritance God set aside for you, His beloved. Essentially, a new generation of Kingdom agents has been produced as an answer to the spiritual frustration that many Christians have been sensing. You are in the right place for God to catapult you headlong into your destiny, purpose and your identity in Him. You are part of a generation that seeks to pursue and live out their Kingdom purpose; a generation of Daniels, Josephs, and Esthers; a Kingdom generation.

The K-Gene traces the lineage of this current Kingdom generation, and motivates their future course of action. If you are tired of church-as-usual, and can feel the pull for more, then you might just have come to the reality that the K-Gene resides within you. Welcome to your new day of realized purpose and fulfillment! You are a Kingdom asset, and we've been awaiting your arrival!

This book seeks to bring definition, clarity, inspiration, and affirmation to this new generation. The K-Gene will provide an understanding of the systems that help illuminate and broaden your horizons of development within this Kingdom realm – a realm that we are all surely affected by. Proverbs 4:7 admonishes the believer to not only obtain wisdom, but also understanding. Based on its Hebrew root word *bin*, understanding (*binah*) denotes the ability to rightly discern attained information and successfully execute its application. This book will provide a few of many

Kingdom concepts that are meant to be walked out. These principles must become habitual, a lifestyle change, in order to successfully unlock the genetic information of the Kingdom that lies dormant inside each of us. This book may pique the interests of the inquisitive, but it will only satisfy the truly hungry who are willing to change to see God's Kingdom cover the earth in and through them. Kingdom is not just a system, but a way of life … and you have already been genetically wired to reveal God's Kingdom in the earth. I pray that this prophetic teaching develops your character as you journey to become the true manifestation of the sons of God. Enjoy your journey as you activate the dormant Kingdom genetic code that God placed within you! Enjoy unlocking the K-Gene.

ACTIVATING THE K-GENE

CHAPTER 1: KINGDOM

The beginning of all things is God. There is no way to get around this eternal fact, and nothing would exist without Him. To understand a kingdom and its ways, one must first have an understanding of the king. After all, every kingdom thrives off of the identity and mentality of its monarch. The fact that God is the creator of all things also makes Him King, and the presence of a king implies that there is a kingdom. The system of Kingdom existed before the beginning, just as God was before creation. Thus when God made man in His likeness, man was not only a spiritual being but also inherently a Kingdom being. Since God is the King, His Kingdom DNA was genetically passed on to humanity. If there was ever a place where Kingdom gene was placed within man, it was at this point of formation. At the creation of man, the Kingdom Gene, or the K-Gene, was activated and drove the desires and intentions of man into alignment with the will of God.

Adam enjoyed open fellowship with God and a peaceful alignment with everything in nature. Adam resided in God's Kingdom, yet it was the active K-Gene that allowed him to function properly in God's sovereign domain. Adam experienced true peace, dominion in the earth, and synchronized movement with God. It was a time without exploitation or hard labor, because Adam maintained the Garden as a love fellowship with God. Yes, man had choice and free will, and as long as he willingly chose to abide in obedient synchronization with God the K-Gene remained active. This constantly placed Adam in fulfilled interactions with his King. This was the perfect state of being for humanity, where every need was met and there were no vulnerabilities — except for the gift of free will. And it was this vulnerability that eventually made man accountable for the fall from grace.

To characterize the fall as simply eating forbidden fruit is a huge oversight on the part of the believer. This fall was not just a mere "fall from grace" as we often like to annotate it, but a drop from a higher state of living, thinking, and acting, to a lesser state. The fall was a battle of systems, a contest of two prevailing ideologies, a choice that needed to be made by humanity. The choice was between God's superior Kingdom system and the inferior system of man's self-image. Consider the argument that the subtle serpent makes to Eve in the Garden. It begins with a thought meant to cause Adam to take the future into his own hands. First, the serpent twists God's Kingdom decree in conversation with Eve, with the sole intention of distorting her perception of the reality of things. "Yea hath God said, 'Ye shall not eat of every tree of the

garden ... Ye shall not surely die" (Genesis 3:1-4 KJV).

The serpent gets into a proverbial duel with Eve over

whether the eating of the fruit meant assured death. Eve

was attempting to combat the logic of the serpent with

Adam's first-hand experience of God's decree, not her

own experience. Perhaps this is why some of us

similarly find ourselves in continuous cycles of failure,

despite the countless Christian conferences and decreed

and declared biblical rhetoric over our lives.

Experiences with God must be personal, and God's

Word must be digested to be of adequate use to the

hearer. You can't expect that you'll overcome by

someone else's testimony, nor will you be able to

withstand crafty demonic logic without knowing the

Word for yourself.

The serpent's argument was subtle enough to

dissuade Eve from God's system of logic, for it was

crafted with a mixture of God's Word and personal feelings. "You shall surely die" … this was the promise of God to Adam. The same words that the enemy used against Eve. After eating the fruit, Adam and Eve did not drop dead physically. No, they lived a long life that would make all of our years small in comparison. So did God lie? Was the enemy correct that they wouldn't die, but would rather flourish like their Diety? The truth is that they misunderstood what God meant when He spoke of death.

God is a Spirit, so any command and penalty that He gives has a spiritual component. Therefore, the death that God spoke of was spiritual, which is why Adam and Eve's mortal bodies were not immediately affected, but at the moment of transgression they experienced a spiritual separation. The serpent's real intent with his argument was to prompt Adam to construct a self-image. "For God doth know that in the day *ye* eat thereof, then *your* eyes shall be opened, and *ye* shall be as gods, knowing good and evil." This logic seems harmless on the surface, yet in a Kingdom system the emphasis is more on the King than on the subjects. In the beginning, Adam did not do anything for himself, nor was his motive to improve upon his status and reputation. His work in the Garden was as an act of worship unto his Creator. The constant fellowship that Adam sought was attributed to his genuine love for God. Now suddenly the serpent introduces Adam and Eve to the concept of self-determination. Instead of working as worship of their king, they now worked to build an empire for themselves. Worship had been perverted by Lucifer, and now he had caused man to pervert the Kingdom covenant that they held with God.

Kingdom is a system of trust and covenant between rulers and their subjects. The subjects willingly obey the laws of the land and work communally for the

greater good of the kingdom and their monarch. In

return, the king looks out for the security and provision

of the citizenry. Everything in kingdom is about the

king, and every action is done for the furtherance of the

collective kingdom. With his reasoning, the serpent

succeeded in convincing man to become self-driven

instead of Kingdom-driven. When Eve presents Adam

with the fruit, the reality is that his choices were

between two opposing systems: God's image for man,

and man's self-constructed image of himself. So when

Adam chose to eat of the fruit of the tree of knowledge

of good and evil, man's self-image was constructed.

And it was constructed in a way where we became the

primary caretakers of our body, soul, and spirit. After

that, the prevailing culture was to look out for "Number

1,"; self-preservation at all costs, consistent entrapment

to building and maintaining the images we would separately create for ourselves.

We create the monsters that we see and the dark characters that we have become. Your greatest enemy is not the devil, nor is it your "haters," but it's the image you created for yourself. So now everything that man does is in line with sustaining the imagery that we designed. We lie, cheat, steal, and degrade other people's character ultimately because it is all part of our master plan of self-identity and self-preservation. Adam introduced a genetic disorder into humanity, which would display itself through various sinful actions and motives.

A genetic disorder is a disease or illness that is a direct result of an abnormality in the genes, and this disorder is often present at birth. An abnormality is a deviation from the normal function of things, or a perversion of the original intent. When Adam ate the fruit, his disobedience ushered sin into the world and all humanity was now born with this genetic disorder. This is why David could then rightly assert that he was "born into sin, and shaped in iniquity." Adam's paternal Kingdom chromosomes were immediately put to sleep, and all that remained were his maternal instincts (that of the natural, mother earth, our fleshly desires). In essence, the K-Gene still existed within Adam and Eve, but was rendered temporarily inoperative. Though he would never realize it, Adam needed help because he had turned into a monster by accepting a false reality.

Although there was now a genetic disorder ushered into the earth, God's commands to be fruitful, multiply, and replenish the earth were not repealed. Thus man began to reproduce after his kind, complete with the inherent desire to build and protect our own self-constructed images. There is something to be said about using our own methodologies to implement God's power and commands, as these scenarios always turn out to be disastrous. Have you ever tried to do what you believed God commanded you to do, but carried it out in your own understanding and ideology? The results are not far from that of David's disappointment when his attempts to bring back the Ark of the Covenant resulted in Uzzah's death (2 Samuel 6:7-8 KJV). Many of us have good intentions and noble ideals, yet if these plans are detached from God's original intent, they are doomed to fail. When man rebelled against God, humanity was still endued with power, but left with a skewed perception that muted our ability to succeed in the Kingdom.

Mankind now attempted to operate in God's system with their self-constructed ideology. Selfishness lived on and was replicated from generation to generation. Adam and Eve gave birth to Cain and Abel, who both present their respective offerings unto the Lord. Abel gives unto the Lord out of faith, while Cain offers unto the Lord through mere works. Abel chooses to operate in faith, which is indicative of not only God's heart, but His way of operating. In essence, Abel executes the correct righteous desires with the correct methodology of operating. Cain gives unto God out of his own human intellect, the best that he can do absent of faith, yet he fails to understand that this offering is inadequate to a perfect God who requires a more excellent sacrifice. He had chosen to try to accomplish the right desires (the desire to sacrifice unto the Lord) through the self-image that he had created. When God refused to favorably accept Cain's sacrifice, his reaction was one of violence and selfishness. He slays his brother Abel, and then answers God regarding his accountability with the statement "Am I my brother's keeper?"

This system of selfishness and elevation of self-images did not stop with Cain. The Tower of Babel was an account of mankind's attempt to collectively build a name for themselves and affront God's command. "And they said, Go to, let us build us a city and a tower, whose top may reach unto the heaven; and let us make us a name, lest we be scattered abroad upon the face of the whole earth." (Gen 11:4 KJV) One of the flaws in the ideology of this collective group was the notion that they could draw near to God and stand before Him with their self-images still standing erect, with their pride in full operation.

The book of Judges is full of accounts where every man was doing what was right in his own eyes. King Saul's plea to Samuel to refrain from exposing him as a fallen king was nothing more than a feeble effort to salvage the broken pieces of his image before the children of Israel. King David's fornication with

Bathsheba, which led to the ultimate order to murder her husband, Uriah, was driven by selfish motives. Yet lest we look at these biblical characters in judgment, we are still producing monstrosities under the name of Christ today. The biggest of these self-made monuments is the "man-made" system of church.

To be clear, church is a system that was orchestrated by God to accomplish His will in the earth. However there has been a perversion of that system, built off the works of the genetic disorder of man. It is this flawed system that people refer to when they say "I was hurt by the church." It is a system that is thoroughly fueled and ignited by the selfish desires of men. Both leaders and laypersons alike are guilty of birthing the man-made monstrosity that has turned people away from a genuine understanding and image of our God. Take an honest look at what we've instituted as the general understanding of church. It is built off of satisfying the fleshly appetites of the congregants, or pushing the agenda of a personality. Unfortunately, some congregants have an insatiable hunger for entertainment and amusement, so we pick churches based on cosmetic parameters: what a church has externally instead of what it is doing for us internally. Therefore, the man-made system of church produces nothing greater than a circus experience that temporarily dazzles us away from our troubles, but does not empower us to live life victoriously after the show ends. We are drawn to churches based on who has the best music ministry, who has the most charismatic preachers, the largest congregations, or the most innovative technological advances. We pick churches because our friends go there, or our family members were founders of the church.

Unfortunately, when these things change, we move to another church and never learn the power of being planted or settled. We leave churches because people

offend us, we feel underappreciated, we aren't being

elevated fast enough, or we had a disagreement with the

pastor. In order to keep members in seats, pastors feel

forced to preach on *our* issues, for fear that we will lose

focus, become disengaged, and leave. So we end up

with many Christians who are spiritually nomadic,

wandering from place to place and suffering from

instability.

On the other end of the spectrum, the man-made

church has sadly produced some pastors and leaders

whose appetites are their god. They place their public

image and success above to the needs of the sheep that

they are responsible for shepherding. They have the

degrees, the business models, and the charismatic

personality of a pastor, but they lack the heart and mind

of God concerning His sheep. They hold an improper

perspective on the system of church. Each side blames

the others, laypeople versus leaders, yet the truth is that we are all responsible for the perversion of God's church system. So out of this genetic disorder of sin, selfishly driven people constructed a version of church that was all about humanity instead of being all about the King.

Alcoholics Anonymous is renowned for its foundational maxim: admitting that you have a problem is the first step to recovery. I believe that most of us can readily admit that we have a problem, but when it comes to taking responsibility for being the cause of the messes in our lives, we fall short. The truth is that humanity will always be in the same position that Adam and Eve were in at the beginning: one choice away from both success and failure. So often we blame the devil and his demonic team for our downfall, or we throw the blame on the people around us, on the church, and on society. The reality is that God has given to each of us the ability to choose for ourselves.

Satan made a tempting argument to Eve, but she *chose*

to eat the fruit, as did Adam. "The devil made me do it"

has become a convenient distraction from the reality

that our flesh really wanted to experience whatever we

desired, and we chose to satisfy our thirsts. You will

never truly be free from the bondage of sin if you don't

acknowledge that you were the gatekeeper who decided

to let your environment be what it is.

Some of the most liberating conversations that I've

had with God have started with me confessing to God

that there was really a part of me that wanted to fulfill

the thought or action that I enacted. "God, I looked at

pornographic images because I wanted to, and although

the devil suggested it, I chose to yield to that advice."

"God, my family was murdered and I was rightfully

angry, yet I chose to take on hatred in my heart for the

murderer because I believed it was the only way I could

get true resolution of this tragedy." You see, in every position, whether it is an action or reaction, our choices allow or dismiss whatever forces wish to influence our lives. Some of us need to admit not only that we have a problem, but also that our choices got us where we are. The freedom in admitting that your circumstances are a product of your choices is this simple truth: if you created the self-image then you also have the power to destroy it.

Living in Kingdom is a rejection of self-determination, and an acceptance of letting our Sovereign King, God, provide for us. The key to the fulfillment of all things is Kingdom, which can only be accessed through Jesus Christ. Kingdom is not just a term, but a way of life and a system that leads us into total dependence on God. People who buy into any kingdom system should enjoy protection and provision by the ruling monarch or entity. This is why Christians are encouraged to seek the Kingdom of God (God's sovereign rulership), and His righteousness (God's way of living and thinking). Being in proper alignment is everything to Kingdom success. If you are not willingly living a life that is submitted to God's sovereignty, then you will never receive Kingdom benefits.

Before you continue reading this book, right now would be a great time to evaluate your pattern of decisions to get to the foundation of the self-image that you've constructed. The reactivation of the K-Gene within you will bring the disclosure of your purpose, true peace, fulfillment, and the stability you so desperately desire to own. The first step to reactivation is the destruction of your own image and the acceptance of God's Kingdom will for your life. Who is willing to press the self-destruct button and allow God to unlock the true potential that has always resided in you from the beginning? Who is willing to embark on the journey of the unknown, to step out of the boat of all that you find familiar and step onto the raging sea of your next dimension in God. Who is willing to declare, "God, I trust You"? This is the place where everything that you have built in your old way of thinking must be discarded, and like Abraham you move to the place of God's leading. Let the mask that you've hidden behind fall, because it is time for the real you to shine forth! God sets before you both life and death — please choose life. It is time that you choose Kingdom!

NOTES OF REFLECTION

CHAPTER 2: THE K-GENE

Gene /jeen/ (n.): a unit of heredity composed of DNA or RNA and forming part of a chromosome, etc., that determines a particular characteristic of an individual. (gene n.d.)

Genetics (n.): The study of heredity and the variation of

inherited characteristics. (genetics n.d.)

You have been genetically wired to be like God. When God created humanity, we were created in His image and likeness. He wanted us to look and act like Him. You have a pre-existing condition that was placed inside you far before you entered the world. Yes, you were born in sin and shaped in iniquity, however, God placed His Kingdom genetics within you before you came into existence in this earth. Think about that for a moment. We often think of God as an invisible being that is on the sidelines of life rooting for us. We know that He sent His Son, Jesus Christ, to level the playing field by dying for our sins. Yet what we don't all realize is that God also embedded a genetic code within us to ensure victory should we choose Christ as Lord and Savior. God didn't just form you, He personally invested Himself into you. You have a direct connection with your Creator! This is a connection that allows us to function on earth as God does in Heaven. In essence, since the beginning of time God has never simply stayed on the sidelines, but He has actively gotten into the game for all those who would willingly accept His help.

The study of genetics is a pertinent undertaking as it holds vital information regarding our identity, behavior patterns, and future potential. Genes provide the blueprint to the body, instructing cells on when and how to function. I would submit that, just as there are natural genes, Kingdom has a genetic makeup. These K-Genes, derived from God, help us desire, seek, and attain spiritual things. Paul declares that there is a "good that I would do." There are godly desires and pursuits that lie within each human being, something that drives us to do better, be better, and act better. This component is not some outward Jiminy Cricket, no external voice that dictates and drives our moral compass, but rather an internal yearning.

It is important that we realize that the K-Gene came first. Before all of our hang-ups, life's hiccups, and our short-comings, the K-Gene was deeply embedded into our identities. This means it is not just what you do, but who you are. That is why Paul could express frustration over the "good that he wanted do" although sin seemed to be the end result. From the most pious saint to the "worst" sinner, we have a natural desire to do what is right in God's eyes. We have the internal instinct to want to please God. However, without Christ, we are not able to authentically act upon these Kingdom urges. Placing the K-Gene within you was not accidental nor coincidental. Original intent and precedence matters to God, so He intentionally equipped you with this blueprint for success prior to everything else that life would entail. In doing this, God ensured that you would always have a reference point that could be useful should you deviate from the path.

Proverbs 22:6 is a scripture that we often recite to anxious parents who worry about the potential detours that their kids may take in the future. It states: "Train up a child in the way he should go: and when he is old he will not depart from it." Parents should embed good teaching and sound doctrine in their children during their most formative and impressionable years. Doing so gives them something foundational to hold on to when faced with many different voices and choices in life.

The word "train" in this context means to initiate, consecrate, and inaugurate. In other words, it is the responsibility to initiate and preempt any future life encounters with solid teaching that can serve as a guide through difficult seasons. This is what Daniel's parents did for him. Prior to Babylonian captivity, Daniel's parents made sure that they adequately trained him in the laws of the Lord. Daniel allowed this to become his meditation, as he would recite it when he arose from sleep and when he sat down to eat. His parents secured Daniel's pathway to success by promoting an environment of godly thinking and living. I'm sure they never imagined that Daniel would be separated from them so early in life. Yet, they had nothing to worry about because they had set a precedent within Daniel and positively affirmed his K-Gene. As a result, God was not concerned when Babylonian teaching became a requirement for all captives, because His Word preempted any teachings that Daniel would receive in the future. The only way Daniel could fail was by conscientiously rejecting and exchanging the true teaching he had received for another doctrine.

What was done for Daniel is also true regarding your life with God. He strategically endued you with the genetic code, to give you a reference point that could guide you to Himself. The sole reason that we desire God, though we sometimes fill that void with other things, is because He designed us to do so. Before the invaluable gift of Jesus Christ, God gave you another gift to ensure that you would always have a way to be connected with your Kingdom heritage. He gave you the K-Gene.

The K-Gene stands for Kingdom genetics. You have within you the code of conduct of Kingdom. You have the blueprint to all things God inside of you. Righteousness, peace, prosperity, security, life … these qualities lie within you, given to you by God. Each person has the K-Gene within, however, due to the effects of sin humanity's K-Gene has generally been muted. Inactivity of this gene should never be mistaken for absence. So where exactly is this K-Gene that we possess?

It is first worth recalling the fact that we are triune beings like our Creator. Our existence comprises of three parts: body, soul, and spirit. Your Kingdom genetics are specifically linked to your spirit man. Your spirit is the part of you that is like God; it is your connection to our King. God is a spirit, and as such He communicates with our spirit man. Spirit interfaces with spirit, soul with soul, and flesh with flesh. Your spirit desires spiritual things, your soul desires soulish things, and your flesh craves material things. This principle is scriptural and holds true. When you try to

fulfill spiritual desires with fleshly things it never

satisfies because these two components have specific

tastes and needs. Your spirit hears the voice of God,

captures the sounds of Heaven, and enjoys fellowship

with the Maker of the Universe. Your soul and flesh

can only feel the effects of these connections, but your

spirit receives the full experience.

When God carries out transactions, they are

spiritual in nature. Furthermore, since God is a spirit,

His Kingdom is inherently spiritual. The Kingdom of

God is a spiritual truth that eventually manifests

naturally through the hearts and actions of men. Your

spirit is the only part of you that can fully conceptualize

Kingdom things. When Jesus admonishes us to seek

first the Kingdom of God and His righteousness, He is

referring to spiritual pursuits. As God is King, and

Kingdom is spiritual, then it would logically follow that

the spirit realm is the highest realm. Spirit trumps all

things … everything initiates from a spiritual place and

then eventually manifests naturally. Prior to sin, God's

original intent was for man to dwell and rule from a

spiritual place. Yes, we live in the flesh, but we were

meant to reside and reason spiritually. There was a

hierarchy that God designed to help man regulate

himself. In the ideal system, your spirit man stays in

constant communication with God. Your spirit then

relays the appropriate message to your soul, and then

your soul gives direction to your flesh. For example,

your spirit man may hear God instruct you to give

financially. Your spirit then tells your emotional state

(soul) to get ready to give cheerfully. Your soul then

relays the message to your flesh to give. This is how

you live from a spiritual place, or from the inside out.

In this systematic set up, your K-Gene is unhindered.

Because Kingdom is spiritual, your genetic blueprint for Kingdom (your K-Gene) is housed within your spirit. When Adam and Eve rebelled, they exchanged God's voice for self-determination. This produced a warped system that could not compare with the benefits that we received within God's system. For one, our spirit man ceased to hear from God at the same open rate, due to the barrier of sin. Because our spirit was no longer hearing from God, it was no longer giving instructions to the soul. This absence of instructions from spirit left soul to follow the directions that were produced out of self-determination, leaving flesh gratified (and out of control). When our spirit man ceased to fellowship continuously with God, our K-Gene was muted ... left with an inability to express itself. In essence, man continued to live life on earth, but was bereft of the title deed to the Kingdom inheritance that was rightfully ours.

After centuries of awkward silence between God and humanity, Jesus steps on the scene with a timely message: "Kingdom is at hand!" His first announcement was not about His arrival, but about the return of Kingdom. As the Son of God, Christ is not only the door to open fellowship with the Father, He is also the door to Kingdom. Through Christ, we are able to enjoy constant fellowship with God, which means that we are empowered anew to live life from the inside out. Our spirits are now able to assert authority and influence over our souls and flesh, resulting in lives that are completely aligned with Kingdom. Only through the acceptance of Jesus Christ as Savior can we reactivate the K-Gene. Christ is the fulfillment of all things, and His purpose was to bring us back into reconciliation with God and with our destiny in Him. Your K-Gene has the power to bring you in direct alignment with your inheritance. Activating this gene

should be the priority of every Christian believer.

NOTES OF REFLECTION

CHAPTER 3: HELP! I'VE CREATED A MONSTER!

Who am I? Why do I exist? What is my purpose in life? If you live long enough, you will eventually ask yourself these questions. Every day, we attempt to do things that will validate our existence, things that give purpose and meaning to all the random experiences that make up life. There is something unsettling feeling like you don't matter, or that what you do has no meaning or value to those around you. We change jobs, our outward appearances, our circles of friends and associations, all under the pursuit for meaning, relevance, and purpose. The answer to your quest for purpose is inside you. It has always been inside you, and there is not one single event or circumstance that could remove it from you. From the very moment you were conceived, you came fully equipped with purpose locked deep within you. Purpose is not some external entity that you chase after, but rather an internal treasure box that you must unlock. Yes, the power, peace, victory, and your identity are all locked up inside you. To avoid humanism, allow me to be very clear in my analysis. Purpose lives in every human being, and it is ripe for the taking. However, you will not be able to successfully unlock this potential without God! Without living a life fully yielded to the Creator of all mankind. Since He is the architect of your purpose and your potential, it will take partnering with Him to understand (1) what power lies within you; and (2) how to adequately use that power. In God's mind, unlocking the K-Gene brings you closer to your full reunion with Him.

What frustrates many believers is that we can perceive what "is right" and we even desire to do it, yet the outward expression of such desires proves elusive even to the best of us. Sadly, many Christians struggle with understanding who they are. How many people in the body of Christ are walking around aimlessly? These people are saved, undoubtedly, yet still disconnected from the understanding of their identity. Essentially, they are heaven bound, but unproductive concerning the Kingdom of God here on earth. This is dangerous in a system where God requires us to produce fruit. Church is filled with many believers who work tirelessly toward the tenets of Christianity with no understanding, no vision, no pathway forward, and no strategy. If there is no understanding of one's identity, then how is one to comprehend their purpose? And if they remain disconnected from their purpose, how will they function properly and move forward? No wonder stagnation abounds in the church today!

To be stagnant means to make little or no advancement. It should be noted that stagnation is not just merely the absence of movement, but lack of a meaningful pace of flow. In essence, one could be moving, but not at a quick enough pace to increase momentum or cause change. The trick of the enemy is to deceive Kingdom citizens into believing that the speed or rate of flow is not important. However, consider water that is collected in a pool, slowly drop by drop. In this example, water is being added, however, the addition is so slow that there is no movement, no change. Eventually this water will smell and become a breeding ground for mosquitos (blood-sucking parasites). If you have found yourself surrounded by blood-draining and life-sucking forces, it could be that you are in this place of stagnation. People who don't know their purpose usually end up with no, or restricted, movement and thus become easy prey to life-draining agents.

Alternately, consider each time Jesus uses the word "water" in connection with believers; it is never described in a stagnant condition. The waters are described as flowing, and usually paired with the word "living" (meaning to be active). Thus, Kingdom citizens are always active and fruitful, moving toward a vision even when they are in a posture of waiting. Life should not be passing you by, because you were genetically predisposed to being mobile and producing meaningful fruit. Perhaps this is the root of the stagnation problem: we don't know our genetics and therefore we don't know our origin, history, vulnerabilities, or capabilities. There is more to you than what people perceive outwardly, and the current trials that you face are a text of the pre-existing conditions you are naturally prone to display. This is why it is important to understand the Kingdom in terms of Kingdom genetics. Genes carry the code, the original the original blueprint for our creation, so any discussion on genetics, inheritances, or lineages must begin at that foundation.

The English name "Genesis," which comes from the Hebrew word *bereshith,* literally translates into "in the beginning." This biblical book is an account of the first of many systems and creations in the earth, including the creation of man. God's creations were all a product of His mind and His imagination. Genesis 1:27 is the account of the creation of humanity. God spoke words that matched His thoughts, as He declared with an assured breath, "Let us make man in our image and likeness." He willed Himself to make man, yet it wasn't only important that man *was* created; *where* man originated was equally important. At this point that you might expect me to solely focus on the words "image" and "likeness," yet equally important in this context is the word "made." You see, the word "made" in the Hebrew (*asah)* implies the act of bearing or bringing forth. He made you with the inscription of His image and form. God called forth the lights, the trees, the animals, and the land mass; yet when He made humanity He brought us forth from His mind. So our place of origin was the realm where God dwelt, eternity. In fact, when God decrees that man would be made in his image and likeness, He was referring to making Him as a spiritual being outside of time and in eternity. Therefore, yes, we do look like God, but this does not mean that our flesh or outward exterior is a reflection of God. God is not a race, ethnicity, or gender, but God is a Spirit (John 4:24) and interactions with Him must be spirit to spirit. This is why your primary state of being, and the part of you that is like God, is your spirit-man.

When we were first created, we were created as spiritual beings. Then, God formed us from the dust of the ground, which gave us a body. Finally, He breathed the breath of life in us, and man became a living soul. Genesis 2:7 is actually an account of man becoming a three-dimensional being: body, soul, and spirit, of which spirit is supposed to have pre-eminence in the inner system of each person. This is why Paul encourages us to "walk in the spirit," or "live in the spirit," or "but rather desire spiritual things"; he is pointing to the fact that the spiritual side of you is the authentic you, your first state of being. It is your spirit that is eternal, the part of you that was here before your body and soul, and this spirit will live on after your body physically dies.

God spoke humanity into existence, with the original intent that man would enjoy the benefits and responsibility of being made in His very image and likeness. We've already determined that the image of God is our spirit man; however, it is His likeness that is the "genetic" link between God and humanity. Likeness means that the progeny shares the characteristics, traits, and mannerisms of their genetic predecessors. Have you ever heard the phrases "you are just like your mother" or "you act just like your daddy"? When people express this sentiment, they are not necessarily talking about your outward appearance, but your conduct or behavior. The funny thing is that you don't have to be in the presence of your parents to act out their tendencies; in fact, you don't even have to really know them to behave like them. The genetic bond that you share eventually displays itself over the course of your life no matter how hard you attempt to suppress it. The same is true with your creator, God. You may not be able to see Him, hear Him, or even currently know Him, yet He placed His Kingdom Gene inside you. At the moment that God decided that we would be made in His likeness, He simultaneously gave us our K-Gene. And even though you try to suppress it, the truth is that there is a continuing war going on inside of you, between who *you* want to be and who God made you to be.

A battle of competing images and consciousness play tug of war with your mind and your spirit so that you are constantly conflicted about how to move or operate. You feel pulled in many different directions at once, which ultimately leads you to try to search for anything that will give you peace and make the conflict cease. This same conflict exists for non-Christians. Try as they might to cover up their genetic connection to God, they find themselves unfulfilled and empty, while the desires and urges of their Creator live on inside of them. This cry for fulfillment is voiced by the unsaved and the redeemed alike, although those who are redeemed are closer to the place of resolution. This cry is specifically for the Kingdom of God to be manifested in and through us.

I am a depraved monster seeking self-gratification and so are you ... well, at least we used to be, if we now indeed have had our natures changed by Jesus Christ. Paul said it best when he admitted that "no good thing dwells in our flesh." The monsters that we have created, and thus become, are not always the product of ill will, or some diabolical plot. In fact, many people find themselves in these unfortunate quandaries due to a universal pursuit: security. It is natural to want to ensure ourselves and to feel that everything is taken care of. We pursue houses, cars, and land because we despise the sense of being insecure. Insecurity is a very unnerving feeling that leaves its victims paralyzed. It's not just simply people with low self-esteem, but more about the feeling of inadequacy or a deficit in any given area of life. When we stress about our bills, pondering how they will get paid, this is the potential manifestation of insecurity. We are then left at a crossroads, with the responsibility to either choose God's way or go it alone.

Our change into our current state is best described as a process of metamorphosis. It was not a one-time event, but a series of bad decisions. Every time we operated out of fear and handled our problems through self-determination, instead of obedient trust in God, we coddled the K-Gene to sleep and empowered the self-preserving monster. The truth is that living in Kingdom requires a rejection of self-preservation and an acceptance of letting our Sovereign King, God, provide for us. The key to the fulfillment of all things is Kingdom, which can only be accessed through Jesus Christ. Kingdom is not just a label, but a way of life and a system that leads us into total dependence on

God. People who buy into a kingdom system should enjoy protection and provision by the ruling monarch or entity. This is why Christians are encouraged to seek the Kingdom of God (God's sovereign rulership) and His righteousness (God's way of living and thinking). Being in proper alignment is everything to Kingdom success.

Because sin entered into the world, all humanity begins life with a perverted understanding of the original intent God had when He formed us in His image and likeness. Outside of Christ's leading, our self-determination has molded us into monsters with a muted conscience. Sometimes, the combined weight of all of the bad decisions we have made become a burden that seems impossible to lift. We can see a better life, a better self without the current character flaws, a life of freedom, of victory, of hope. We just can't seem to attain to it. Life seems like a daily struggle, an uphill battle to get to God's designated blueprint, a blueprint that we can feel rising within us every now and then. How do we get to that person? How do we get to that place? One word: reconciliation!

Reconciliation is defined as (1) the restoration of friendly relations or (2) the action of making one view or belief compatible with another. In essence, we must go through the process of sifting through two diametrically opposed viewpoints (God's and ours) to come to one succinct thought and lifestyle. As Christians, we should acknowledge God as Sovereign Originator, and thus defer to His viewpoint. We become reconciled with the Kingdom of Heaven when we willingly lay down our thought processes and our ways of life in exchange for God's ways and thoughts. Jesus' Kingdom mission was to reconcile us to the Father, which He did by dying on the cross for our sins.

In terms of Kingdom, I have come to understand that reconciliation is a two-fold process: salvation and sonship, or put in other terms, making Jesus Savior *and* Lord of our lives. Reconciliation begins by accepting the free gift of Jesus Christ, which is salvation. He truly is the doorway to redemption, and His task was to reconcile us back to God. Without accepting Christ as our Savior, we are incapable of igniting the Kingdom Gene that lies within us, and we are unable to deconstruct the monsters that we have built. Yes, salvation is key! However it is only the beginning of God's ultimate plan for us. God's intent was much broader than simply forgiving us of our sins. That is why grace must be celebrated not just for its redemptive qualities, but also its empowering abilities.

The fullness of God is to undo the self-made man that we built, reignite the K-Gene within us, and bring us to a place where we are reigning victoriously in the earth. This last stage is known as sonship. Have you ever wondered what life was like prior to Adam and Eve's transgression? Have you ever considered what the purpose of humanity was, and what we gained when God created us? This divine transaction was man's introduction into sonship. Adam enjoyed a direct connection with his Father and Creator. He was directly endued with power and responsibility by God, and he wanted for nothing. What classified this place as sonship was that God intended for the earth to be the inheritance of His greatest creation, humanity.

Earthly kings leave a legacy for their children to grow into and ultimately rule on their behalf. When princes are first born, they are heirs of their father's possessions. Every time the king increases in status, wealth, or territory, the sons are the beneficiaries of those achievements. Yet in order to possess what is rightfully theirs, princes must grow into the king's legacy. Like other princes, you may feel inadequate, as if the space that you are called to is much bigger than your ability to handle it. Take a deep breath and relax. No prince was born with all the answers; other than Jesus Himself, no child was born perfect. Maturity is a process, and God designed this life's journeys to develop you from a prince to a fully functioning king. It's no coincidence that life's problems sometimes seem overwhelming and knock you to your knees in prayer. The process is working best at these times because it is reconciling you with God's way of thinking.

It is possible to be saved but not achieve the sonship that God desires for us. Full reconciliation starts at redemption and ends at reigning. Through salvation, you are reconciled with God; through sonship you are reconciled with His power and legacy (your inheritance). When you are aligned with God to the effect that, through His power within you, you are in control of your emotions, your time, your day, your realm, and your purpose, then you are reigning. This is the highest achievement in sonship.

When God formed and fashioned humanity, there were certain genetic privileges that were inherently part of our makeup: (1) a benefit unto the earth; (2) the power to speak things into existence; (3) a life of abundance and ready-made resources; (4) harmony and unity with the environment both naturally and spiritually; (5) open and unending fellowship with God; (6) the ability and capacity to multiply ourselves (replication); and (7) authority or dominion. I believe that God intends for man to pursue each of these privileges during our time on earth. Mastery of these privileges could make the difference in deconstructing the monstrous identities that we created, and being fully restored to our place of sonship in God's Kingdom.

Only when we willingly lay aside our right to self-

determination and take on the mentality of God will we

be able to truly activate and support the K-Gene that

lies dormant within us.

THE K-GENE 64

NOTES OF REFLECTION

CHAPTER 4: THINK AGAIN!

We live in a highly technological and rapidly paced world, defined as the Information Age. The old adage "knowledge is power" has held consistently true throughout the ages, particularly in our time. Decades ago, it took researchers days or months to gather, review, and download necessary information. Now, at the click of a mouse, knowledge can be quickly attained in mere seconds. With the technology that we have today, information is easily exchanged in the global market, allowing movements and revolutions to evolve almost instantaneously.

On December 17, 2010, Mohammed Bouazizi set himself on fire in Tunisia, and within weeks revolutions broke out in countries all across the Arab world. Egypt's successful overthrow of Hosni Mubarak has been credited to young Egyptians who were able to harness the power of social media to quickly rally support both domestically and internationally, in their fight against oppression. Those examples from 2010 are examples of a common human trait: it is a byproduct of our humanity for us to become wrapped up in the pursuit of new methods, technologies, and capabilities.

However, there is a latent truth that often has been overlooked: there is still power in thought and intellectual ingenuity. Despite humanity's great technological advances, there is no power on earth greater than the human mind. This is especially true when it is operating at its full potential. The kernels of everything that exists on the earth are thoughts. Whether it is a blender, a television, a hospital, or a major revolution, everything that is manifested here is a product of someone's mind. Thoughts, ideological frameworks, and logical patterns rule and regulate the earth and its systems. So, if thoughts are the seeds of everything that exists, then thinkers might stand the greatest chance of ruling the world. It's the people who harness and innovatively implement the transactions of thoughts and ideals who end up being the trendsetters and controlling the flow of society. Their power and influence might not be visible, and they might not be the face of leadership that people see, but society is bound by the systems of their imaginations.

As a comic book fan, I was always intrigued by the rivalry between Superman and Lex Luthor. Superman, the champion of Metropolis, was nearly invincible. He was described as being faster than a speeding bullet, fireproof, and possessing supernatural strength. Parallel to this was Lex Luthor's notoriety as a brilliant criminal, whose strength lay in his ability to mentally master others; hence, the term "mastermind." He was a master of minds, a master of the realm of thoughts and ideals. Their rivalry was the classic battle of brains

versus brawn. I can distinctly remember tuning in to the

television week after week, to see Superman defeat Lex

Luthor and his henchmen. We would all applaud when

Superman saved the day once again. However, there

was a subtle punch line to the rivalry between

Superman and Lex Luthor that I missed for many years.

For all the strength and the physical mastery that

Superman possessed, he was still not on the same plane

as Lex Luthor. I know that I've just made some comic

book enthusiasts upset, but at least consider my ideas

about this. Superman, and the people of Metropolis,

relied solely on this hero's strength as his sole method

of defeating the villain. However noble this may be,

Superman would never develop the ability to outthink

Lex Luthor; never took the time to outsmart the

mastermind, and as such was always subject to being a

reactionary fighter. While Lex Luthor was hiding away

somewhere, or terrorizing the citizens of Metropolis, Superman was stuck continuously fighting the products of Lex Luthor's mind.

Furthermore, Lex Luthor had a distinct advantage over our beloved hero. While Superman could only pass on his capabilities genetically, Lex Luthor had the capacity to leave his philosophy in the minds of millions of people at any given time, ensuring that the legacy of his thoughts would outlast the heroic sacrifices of his foe. Superman was doing one-on-one transactions while Lex was making generational transfers. In essence, The Man of Steel could only temporarily stop the product of Luthor's mind, but Superman lacked the power to destroy Luthor from the root.

So it is with many people today, who attempt to fight spiritual problems (ideals and notions) with physical or material solutions. We are no better than

Superman, fighting the symptoms but never getting to the root cause. We don't realize that the things we struggle with began as a concept that we retained in our thoughts. We have been slow to truly understand that the battle is fought on a mental plane, and so our attempts only temporarily subdue the problem until the cycle of life resurrects these issues afresh. If we are to rebuild ourselves in Christ, we will have to start at the thought stage.

Everything that exists or has ever existed started as a thought and then became a manifested reality once it was followed with actions. Thoughts become words, and when those words are coupled with actions they becomes realities. In that way, thoughts become something that you can experience, a rule that you can live under. Every nation started with notions and ideals that were spoken aloud and received by a group of hearers. The founders then coalesced these notable ideals into written constitutional proclamations that would eventually become the reality that citizens live by. Whether you are driving a car, sitting at your desk, or watching television, you are currently living out someone else's expressed ideal or word. God expressed words in the beginning. It was called "creation" and man still lives in God's reality. Adam and Eve accepted the leadership and doctrine of the devil, and as a result we were adopted into this new warped reality.

God gave us free will. This freedom to choose comes with the responsibility to be accountable for our corresponding actions. We therefore are responsible for the self-images that we've constructed. We were the co-laborers and architects of the systems that ensnared us. For far too long, the enemy has used this truth as ammunition against us. As the accuser of the brethren, he excels in selling us the memories of our failures. However, there is another side to this truth. The fact that you were an architect in this devastating system makes you the most qualified to destroy it. You know the way the system works and through Christ you can exploit its weaknesses and reinstitute God's Kingdom system.

It is impossible for God's Kingdom image for us and our self-images to coexist. One of these images must die for the other to fully live and give us the benefits that are provided by that identity. While we can destroy the image that we built, we don't have the power by ourselves to reactivate the identity that God has for us. Remember, it was your acceptance of a flawed system (thoughts, words, and actions inspired by sin and the kingdom of darkness), that placed you in the current cycle you are in, and it will take a greater system (thoughts, words, and actions inspired by God's righteousness and His Kingdom), to stop these cycles and propel you into your God-given future. Thank God that our K-Gene responds to God-inspired words and scriptural knowledge. In fact, it is better to say that the K-Gene gives us an appetite for God's Word. When the K-Gene is activated within us as believers, we become hungry for the Word of God. Whether it comes through hearing His voice or immersing ourselves in the Scriptures, Kingdom agents desire to be surrounded by God and His Word.

Because thoughts rule and regulate life in this world, then thoughts are the gateways to your next level of growth. This is what true repentance is about, readjusting your thinking. We have built a Christian culture that views repentance in terms of tears, regret, and altar calls. Yet, how many times have we displayed these emotions, only to carry out the very same actions that got us into trouble in the first place? Repentance is not just about regretting an action that you have taken, but about realizing that your actions are indeed sinful

and then embracing God's viewpoint on the situation.
Repentance is a mind change, a shifting of your
thoughts to God's way of thinking. For the believer,
repentance is a daily act of shedding beliefs that are not
in alignment with God's Kingdom way, and willingly
adopting His code of conduct. Therefore, it is important
that you learn to seek out and attain new thoughts that
can help you adopt new actions. Do you understand that
changing your mind is the key to changing your level of
growth? You are one thought away from your
breakthrough and the freedom that you richly deserve.
Since the K-Gene is your connection to God, it is also
your gateway to His thoughts. By the Holy Spirit, we
are able to know the mind of God and adopt His
mindset. It is time for you to achieve dominion over
your thought life. It is time for you to think again!

NOTES OF REFLECTION

THE POWER OF BEING

CHAPTER 5: *BE* THE BLESSIING

In the sequence of the creation of man, God carries out

a significant act in the final stage of production — He

blesses them. God was not just blessing Adam and Eve,

but speaking more from the place of eternity. He

blesses all humanity that would later come from the

lineage of this premier couple. We were meant to live

blessed lives. Blessings were not just meant to overtake

us, but to emanate out of our existence. Today, we have

a skewed understanding of the nature of blessings. We

equate blessings with the attainment and accumulation

of material things such as houses, cars, land, and

money. If our measurement of blessing is dependent

upon the possession of material objects, then wealthy

people are blessed, and the impoverished are destitute

of blessings. To pursue this line of thinking would be to

suggest that, per capita, the United States of America is more blessed than the entire African continent. Furthermore, this thought pattern would lead us to proclaim that Qatar was the most blessed nation in the world, as Forbes found it to be the wealthiest nation of all, back in 2012. But these cosmetic measurements are not accurate and do not line up with God's system. Remember, God is a Spirit. As a spiritual being, everything that He declares and releases is initially spiritual in nature, and we will eventually see the visible evidence of His blessings.

The word "blessed" (*barak*) has a dual meaning that is dependent upon who is doing the blessing. When we speak of God blessing someone or something it means to make beneficial. When man is blessing God, it is viewed in the connotation of kneeling in submission or adoration. This duality is noteworthy because of the fact that God cannot be benefited or edified by anyone or anything. As the perfect being, God's character, abilities, and qualities are not dependent on the acknowledgement of men or the accolades that He receives. When we bless God, or rather acknowledge Him in submission, we place ourselves in the proper position to be able to properly function in Him. But when God blessed man, He actually made man to be beneficial. Man was the benefit. God didn't bless the environment; He blessed man and caused mankind to dwell in the earth. The earth was made better because mankind existed in it. The creation by God was improved upon because of the presence of Adam and Eve. Hopefully, it has become evident why our skewed perception of blessings has derailed us and hindered us from functioning properly.

When we come to the understanding that WE ARE BLESSED, and not the material things we seek, then we can function as an improvement to the earth no matter what we have or where we are. Your place of employment should be better because you work there. Your neighbors should be able to know that they are benefitted because you reside in their community. When you moved into the neighborhood, you already possessed the ability to elevate the status of your environment, despite the lack of material resources. The genuine picture of a blessed person is not the Bill Gates' of the world, but the ones in third-world countries or impoverished situations who go into their environment with nothing and make something great of it. This behavior is in proper alignment with what our God did when He spoke the world into existence. He made something beautiful and of high quality out of literal nothingness.

Have you ever stopped to consider why God went through the trouble of inspiring Moses to write about the account of creation that he was not even present to experience? It couldn't be for the purpose of merely having us stand in awe of His wonders, because He is already perfect and cannot be edified nor torn down by the praises or curses of men. Neither is it because God needs a record so the He can remember His past greatest hits. But essentially, He inspired Moses to write Genesis to show us what we had inherited genetically from Him in the beginning. He wanted us to see what was entailed in functioning with the K-Gene in full operation. We are to realize that He made us in His likeness to be a blessing to our communities, environments, and spheres of influence.

God often gives us a command of something to do or implement, and our first response is often "but God I don't have…". Your identity as the blessing was never dependent upon the external resources around you, but on the likeness of God that dwells within you. Take notice that before God gives man any commands or responsibilities, He blesses us (or makes man a blessing). After He blesses us, He puts a demand on us. God can afford to put a demand on us because He has already made us genetically predisposed to rise to the occasion. The principle here is this: God will never put a demand on you that He has not already built you to succeed at. God blesses man (makes us the benefit) and then every command out of His mouth is geared toward us benefitting the earth, living out of the innate ability to win and conquer situations. These commands were: be fruitful (benefit), multiply (benefit), replenish the earth (benefit), subdue the earth (benefit), and have dominion over every other breathing thing (benefit). Your environment is the perfect mirror that reflects whatever you give off. Therefore, you will look around you and see blessings only when you realize that *YOU ARE* the blessing. It is time that you stop putting an undue expectation on your environment by requiring that it take the lead for your change. Instead, you must instruct your environment, giving it commands that allow it to work favorably towards fulfilling God's mandate on your life.

One of the saddest tragedies of humanity is when we underestimate our value. You were meant to be a positive contributor to the earth, and when you do not live up to the expectation, we all feel the impact of the void that is left. It does not take vast amounts of money or financial stability to be a blessing. You don't even need to have the right earthly connections to be blessed. What defines your blessedness is the fact that you were created by God to naturally BE blessed. Having confidence in God's pre-provision for you is the key to comfortably living as a blessing. Remember, your environment is the perfect mirror. Therefore, if what you are broadcasting and living is the factual identity of being a blessing, then blessings have no other course of action but to reflect that and attach themselves to you.

Take this time to step into your natural role as a

blessing to those around you, and to your environment.

Remember to whom much is given, much is required. If

you show yourself faithful to be the blessing, then

blessings will overtake your life. *Be the blessing.*

NOTES OF REFLECTION

CHAPTER 6: *BE* RESOURCEFUL

After God blessed man, His very next words were "be fruitful." (Gen 1:28 KJV) That word "be" simply means "to exist" and when coupled with an action word, it requires us to exist *as* that adjective. After Moses' death, Joshua was left with the daunting task of leading the children of Israel into their destiny. In response to the understandable fear and doubt that was gripping Joshua's heart, the angel of the Lord gives Joshua the command to "be strong and very courageous." (Joshua 1:7) In essence, Joshua was being told to exist as strength and extreme courage: "Joshua, live as if you are the answer to the problem that is tempting you." Sometimes our problem is that we are not authentically living up to who we were designed to be. So, when God told man to be fruitful, He was literally commanding us to exist as resourceful. This was a commission that was supplemental to God's ordinance to be a benefit to the earth. To be fruitful is to be increasingly productive or continuously bearing fruit. God did not design us to be one-time blessings, or static in nature, but rather to be overflowing in productivity. When we say the word "productivity," typically we are referring to the capacity to produce something or the capacity to build something. However, when God uses this term, He means for us to be resourceful.

When I look back over my life, I begin to notice a correlation between God's timing in giving this command, and my capacity to give. According to our finite understanding, it makes the most sense for a demand on our resourcefulness to be presented when we have the capacity to fulfill it. Yet this is almost never how it happens in God's timing. Have you ever noticed that people draw on your ability when you feel the driest ... those times when you feel empty ... your desert place. When you have the capacity to give, no one seems to ask for a loan or for your time. Wait till you run out of materials and watch how quickly the line forms around you. It is the pull and demand on you during these desert spaces in your life that can quickly cause frustration. In most cases, your frustration is not because of the request, but more a response to the timing of the request. As humans, we hate that inability to meet a need or to address demands that we perceive.

Some of you reading this book are experiencing this desert place right now. You proved yourself to be a good steward of God's resources by saving and conserving, and even giving when appropriate. Then life happened, and you found yourself out of resources. Suddenly, you are surrounded by a crowd of people tugging on you for assistance. Why does this always happen at the dry and low points of your life? Because God is trying to teach you to BE resourceful instead of seeking resources. This is the place where, as sons of God, He is putting a demand on His qualities within us, particularly the quality of creativity and resourcefulness.

Adam was productive when he maintained the Garden of Eden, and this was no small feat. Although there is very little biblical detail provided about the size of the Garden of Eden, it is widely believed that it was at least the size of a province or country. When Adam and Eve were first created and given their task of maintaining Eden, they were the only ones on the earth. They had yet to bear children to delegate chores to, or manservants and maidens to tend to the cultivation of their environment. Their staff consisted of just Adam and Eve. How did they manage to take care of this vast territory without the aid of a lawn mower, jet, car, or boat? Perhaps they possessed the ability to move at the speed of thought, arrive where they needed to be at the mere thought of the location. Maybe they could fly. These things we do not know, but what we do know is that God gave them the command to be fruitful, and when they were judged after the fall, it was not because of laziness or unproductive conduct. Adam and Eve fulfilled the work of God bountifully, providing an increased return off of the investment God had entrusted to them. This command to be productive was not only given to Adam and Eve, but God was speaking into the future of humanity. Perhaps that is what is so wrong with laziness and inefficiency — it contradicts God's original intention for mankind.

Have you ever wondered why you feel unnaturally bothered when it seems like you are underperforming? You constantly feel inwardly driven to do better, perform more efficiently, and to operate more succinctly. And when you don't perform at your highest level, it feels like a huge letdown. When God made you in His likeness, the fullness of Himself included productivity both spiritually and naturally. We may not readily realize it, but we produce things constantly. The reality that you are the blessing and your ability to produce fruit are closely linked together. It is time for you to exist as the blessing that you are, pull on the resourcefulness that God placed inside of you, and produce Kingdom fruit in this earth. Prior to you experiencing your desert places, you were created and formed by a God who placed within you all the resources you would need to accomplish His goals. When God made you, He actually gave you a pre-existing condition of resourcefulness and inexhaustibility. The more you become comfortable in your identity in the earth, the easier it is to be productive.

Resourcefulness in the midst of lack is an expression of the Kingdom Gene that lies within us. This ability is a part of your makeup that you inherited from your Creator. When we realize this powerful truth, through the lens of the Kingdom Gene, it will shift how we respond to lack. Lack comes to test your resolve for fruitfulness. Your K-Gene will never be expressed if it is not tested or put under pressure. Take patience as an example. This quality is never expressed until someone tries it, gets on your nerves. Eventually, you develop what is called "long-suffering," or the ability to control your emotions longer before reacting rashly. In the same way, when your fruitfulness is tested by lack, it helps develop your resolve to accomplish God's will with whatever resources you have at hand. This means that resourcefulness is not always characterized by having an abundant quantity of something, but rather knowing how to utilize whatever you have around you to produce God's intent.

So how do we get to this place of existing as resourceful? The answer is to learn to embrace the power of "being." Adam was at his best when he simply existed as God created him to. When we first see Adam, he is naked but unashamed. He had no raw materials in sight, but he was undoubtedly the richest being on the planet. As long as he was properly aligned with God, he had no needs nor feelings of lack. Because God is inexhaustible, Adam and Eve had access to His vast amount of resources as long as they stayed in order. In essence, they had only one job, and that was to just maintain their state of being. When the serpent planted seeds of inadequacy in their minds, they began to chase the pursuit of knowledge to attain "more" without realizing that they already had an inheritance of this "more." The key to being resourceful is to focus on living authentically in line with God's will, desires, and dictates.

Looking back at the title of this chapter provides an important clue. Notice that the word "*be*" is emphatically italicized, while "resources" is not. The truth is that the more we focus on "being" instead of chasing resources, the more we will naturally be resourceful. Our job is to exist in the manner that God has prescribed for us.

Being in the proper position matters to God. As long as Adam and Eve were stewarding over the Garden as a *worship* unto God, all that they would ever need was readily around them. Gold, bdellium, onyx stones … all of these priceless resources were contained within the grounds that they were called to steward. The reality is that, as they remained in perfect alignment with God's intent, they were frequently interacting with these rare and vast resources that they needed. You will never be more resourceful than your ability to yield to God's will for your life. When you are in this place of submission, those who pull on you in your desert season will never be able to truly drain you. Why? Because being in alignment opens you up to the space of grace that God has authorized for your life. God's strength in us is made perfect through our weakness. God's resourcefulness through us is made perfect in our season of "lack." When you are surrounded by a crowd of people who seem to want everything from you, while you feel depleted, take the time to ensure that you are in proper alignment with God's will for your life. This is the place of grace that we were meant to embrace and live out of. No one can determine for you what the proper position is for your life in any given season.

Identifying your proper position is not an answer that can be sought through majority polls or consensus building. No, this key to your life can only be discovered through intimacy with God and consistent fellowship. The more you intentionally dwell in God's presence, the stronger His voice becomes in your life. In fact, this will also lead to more clarity regarding what lies before you. People who concern themselves with fulfilling God's mandate for their lives have no true need to be concerned for their safety or for funding their future. It is time that we learn to embrace this place of vulnerability, as uncomfortable as it is, because grace awaits us here. Stop searching for resources and learn to *be* resourceful in God's earth. God is waiting to reward your consistent fidelity to Him with the things that you need to continue to thrive. We are at God's best for us when we learn to *be* and allow the resources to come to us.

Like the tragedy in the Garden of Eden, the enemy to your *being* actively tries to get you to focus on anything but submission to God's will. The enemy's job is to tempt you with the promise of a quest for more, which he would have you believe can only be gained utilizing your own wits and strength. He tempted Eve to eat of the fruit by appealing to her hunger for more knowledge and a life on the same playing field as God Himself. The truth is that Adam and Eve already possessed the K-Gene within them, yet they aborted the sure thing that they had for a shadowy promise of something "like it." Through the K-Gene, you have the resources you need to thrive and succeed at all times (no matter how big or small the challenge). When you are truly being fruitful, you will learn how to look at a desert place as an opportunity for demonstration of God's power through you as opposed to an obstacle to your destiny. Possessing resourcefulness is one thing, consistently exercising it is a totally different ball game. I have provided a few important tips that can help you combat the enemy of your fruitfulness.

BE CONTENT

If you take a step back and reevaluate the seasons of your life, you will realize that this desert place is not a new place for you. You have seen it before. It is a very familiar place that has shown up every now and then in your life. In other words, it has been its own cycle in your life. You come to the place where you have money and material resources, everything seems to flow naturally, opportunities are abounding. Then the very next season seems to be one where you are living from paycheck to paycheck, barely scraping by, and you have more bills than you have the ability to pay. Eventually if you ride out that cycle, lack then turns back into comfortable abundance, which then reverts back to lack, only to return again to abundance. These are examples of the cycles of life. Realizing this can help you better cope with the situation because it will shape your outlook on your situation. God wants you to learn how to consistently abound, no matter what you are faced with.

Do you remember MacGyver? This 1980s TV character embodied resourcefulness. He could make anything happen and get out of any situation with the least amount of materials. There was no problem too vast for him — he always found a way to accomplish the task. The screenwriters would write impossible scenarios where his very life was in danger, and all he would have at his disposal was a paperclip and a rubber band. Is this scenario far-fetched? Yes, it is, but the main point was still true. His environment had no bearing on his fruitfulness. When the K-Gene within us is activated, we learn that our environment has no bearing on our ability to produce. God is looking for consistency and commitment concerning your fruitfulness. Paul was in this place of fruitfulness when he spoke of abounding in all things.

"I am not saying this because I am in need, for I have learned to be content whatever the circumstances. I know what it is to be in need, and I know what it is to have plenty. I have learned the secret of being content in any and every situation, whether well fed or hungry, whether living in plenty or in want. I can do all things through Him who gives me strength." (Philippians 4:11–13 NIV)

Paul struggled with adjusting to the seasons and cycles of life. However, he overcame his struggle by embracing the principle of contentment. Contentment is the state of accepting whatever God allows. This principle should not be confused with complacency or settling for less. In fact, those who are content are almost never complacent because they are always progressing ahead toward God's mandate. Contentment is about learning to submit to God's sovereignty. Yielding to His leadership and decision-making. Part of contentment is being fine with whatever decision God makes, including whatever resources He determines you need at any given moment.

Often when God gives us a mandate, the natural response is to give Him the list of things we believe we need to accomplish the task. However, a Kingdom mindset allows us to perceive that at the moment the command was given, God already released to us what He deemed appropriate to fulfill His request. When we find ourselves struggling with discontentment, we begin to look outside of God's intent for ways to supplement His provision. Though we don't articulate this verbally, our actions tell God that He is not enough for us. Think about this. The same God who created the heavens and the earth, who provides for us daily, and gives us our mandates, is somehow not powerful enough to fulfill His needs through us?

Paul uses the specific phrase "learned to be content," which means that achieving contentment is a process. As we go through life's cycles of abundance and lack, we gradually arrive at a place where we become content in God. We learn to ride the cycles of life and become consistent and steady in our trust of God's sovereignty. As a result, we eventually arrive at the point where our ability to produce dwells outside our circumstances or environmental conditions. Satisfied people are focused people, and therefore they are productive people. When you learn to be content in God's provision for you, it frees you to focus on achieving His will.

BE COURAGEOUS

One of the strongest tools the enemy uses to disband our fruitfulness is fear. Fear has many angles and ploys, all meant to intimidate you from seizing God's purpose for your life. Putting hesitation and doubt in the mind of its victims, this spirit of fear makes failure seem inevitable. As sons of God, fear usually attacks us by questioning our ability to succeed. Every true son seeks the approval of the father, and does all that he can to maintain the legacy built by the patriarch. Even the slightest notion of being a disappointment is enough to paralyze the potential heir. In essence, we possess a slight sense of hesitation because we don't want to make a devastating mistake. As a son of God, these feelings are natural and healthy. However, the spirit of fear craftily uses these feelings and takes them to the extreme. We become so fearful of making a mistake that we don't take any actions. Fear keeps us from making progress by purporting the lie that progressing would lead to failure, and thus lead us to making a mockery of the legacy God carefully outlined. However, at best this is just a distortion. Remember, you possess the K-Gene, and success is intertwined in your design.

Traditionally, we have taught believers that the antidote to fear is the three-pronged approach of power, love, and soundness of mind. This is true. Power is necessary to give us the strength we will need to overcome fear. Having security in God's perfect love for us casts out all traces of fear. Soundness of mind allows us to reevaluate our situation from God's viewpoint, an outlook that is not distorted by fear and its extremes. Yet, these three characteristics are ones that can be inwardly held without necessarily placing a demand on action. Fruitfulness requires some sort of external and visible expression to reach fulfillment.

This is why, in addition to these three attributes, courage is imperative to withstanding the spirit of fear.

The word "courageous" is used a total of five times in the Bible, and is used in conjunction with a demand for action. After Moses' death, Joshua was tasked with leading the children into their inheritance. This new leader was to take them to their place of fruitfulness. Once he received his commission, God gave Joshua very clear instructions to be strong and very courageous (Joshua 1:7 KJV). When God sent the children to bring down Jericho's walls, an angel appeared to Joshua commanding him yet again to be strong and very courageous. Why? God understands the trepidation and fear that we feel when surrounded by new challenges and unknown territory. Our omniscient Creator knows that the enemy uses fear to paralyze us. This tactic hinders us from taking the obedient steps that lead to our productivity. Yet God does not always remove the presence of fear from our lives, but rather requires us to overcome it and move forward anyway. God promised that He has not given us the spirit of fear. He is not the author of fear, and therefore it does not have the authorization to dwell with you forever. Yet sometimes God will permit fear to remain present in your situation until you courageously defeat its lies with determined and consistent obedient action.

Courage is the ability to move forward despite the odds. In fact, in biblical connotations, a synonym of the word courageous is "fortify." When you are fortifying yourself, you are strengthening yourself to withstand whatever forces you will encounter. When something is fortified, it is best if the infrastructure is either equal to or greater than the anticipated level of attack. We must learn to match the pressure that fear places on us. If the spirit of fear is relentless, you should be just as relentless in your resolve to move forward. If fear is stubborn, you should be equally as hard-headed in your commitment to move forward. The truth is that when faced with a tall task, it is just as likely that you will fail as you will succeed. The bigger truth, however, is that when you take the risk in obedient faith, God's grace matches your courageous actions to bring you the victory. Being courageous is important to existing as a productive Kingdom agent.

BE RESILIENT

Very few people get things right on the first try, and nobody but Jesus got everything right at all times. Resourcefulness calls for taking action, and every now and then we make errors. In addition to that, things don't always go the way we imagined. As Robert Burns wrote, "the best laid plans of mice and men often go awry." Planning is important, and we should do the best we can to have everything in its proper order. But the poet's point was that even plans carried out with proper planning will experience glitches. Kingdom agents must learn to be flexible and resilient. When God takes into account our lives, I believe He looks at two primary things" (1) the status of our heart and (2) the consistency of our pursuit toward Him. God is less concerned with how many times we make mistakes, and more concerned with our resolve to commit to His path. This quality is called "resilience." Unlike God, there is no way that you will get through life without ever making a mistake. However, due to the K-Gene that you have inherited from our Father, success is inevitable for those who trust in Him. If you are living in proper alignment with God, breakthrough is a matter of "when" it will happen as opposed to "if." Those of us who have problems with resilience usually struggle with anxiety. We become anxious because we put a time limit on God's plans for us and a limit on when we must succeed. We do this out of a fear that we will miss important benchmarks in God's plan. Your productivity is sure, you just need to endure the valleys that define your journey.

God never puts a demand on us without first providing the means and method to get there. You may be feeling the pressure to produce, but just know that you were built to *be* fruitful. When you learn to just exist out of your K-Gene heritage (*be*), every resource will be compelled to follow the God who is in you. The K-Gene empowers us to exist as the fruitful and resourceful beings that our Creator intended for us to be. You are connected to an inexhaustible God who will never allow you to fall prey to lack. It is time that you take the limits off of the God in you. Allow the K-Gene to thrive in you. *Be* resourceful!

NOTES OF REFLECTION

CHAPTER 7: BE PLANTED

Have you ever questioned why you are where you are?
I mean geographically … why this house,
neighborhood, state, nation, or even family? God is the
epitome of perfection. This means that nothing that
God does is arbitrary or accidental. God is very
intentional in all of His movements. His deliberate
actions didn't stop at forming you, but they involved
every detail of your life, including where He planted
you. You are where you are because God planted you
there. Kingdom people understand the importance of
planting and being planted. It is a dangerous path to
roam from place to place under self-determination. You
know what I'm referring to. The place where you set
yourself. Some of us connived, lied, and fought our
way to where we wanted to be, only to lose our

position, status, and credibility. Why? Because you planted yourself and were unable to sustain your productivity. Planters are always responsible for sustaining the proper conditions for the seed, including constant provision. When we plant ourselves, under self-determined conditions, we are obligated to continue to find ways to sustain our presence in that place. I have come to understand that some people are frustrated with their neighborhood, employment situation, and even their church because they planted themselves without understanding this principle of self-determination.

When we attempt to plant ourselves, we also often hold a skewed perception of our source. We expect the job to provide for us, or the church to satisfy our "itch." However, if we planted ourselves in these places, then it is our responsibility, and not these institutions, to fulfill our needs. How many times have we put undue pressures and expectations on systems that were never meant to serve as a source? When will we come to the point where we wait on God and allow Him to plant us where we need to be? When God plants us in a place, He is obligated to sustain us in that environment until He determines that we should be planted in another. The K-Gene within you desires stability in placement. This type of stability can only be attained when we relinquish our drive for self-determination and allow God to plant us in the place He needs us.

The interesting thing about planting is that the seeds don't get to choose where they will be positioned. The determined location of embedding is left up to the sole discretion of the planter. Planters have the advantage of the holding the broadest viewpoint and they can see the bigger picture. Therefore, they are more suited to plant the seeds in their proper, productive place, compared to the random planting of the plants (or the seeds) themselves. Planters consider both the best location and the best time to embed seeds in the ground. Seeds planted under today's conditions might find themselves unprepared for future seasonal patterns and changes. As our planter, when God embeds us in a place, He has considered both our present needs and our future seasons. He knows the bigger picture and strategically plants us in the place where we will thrive the most, both now and throughout life's seasonal shifts.

While God is concerned about us thriving, He also considers where we will be most beneficial to our environment. Remember, each one of us is a revelation of God wrapped in flesh. We each show a different side of God, and we are wired with certain specifications to produce certain very specific things. This means that God usually plants us where there is a deficit or deficiency of the specific thing that we carry. It is a common misconception that our place of planting is where we are accepted and understood. God has the most need of you where there is a void of the Kingdom revelation that you possess. He often plants you in a place to change the way that people live and think regarding God and His Kingdom. Change is almost never received well initially, nor are the people around you able to instantly understand your value, because it has not registered on their radars before. They have nothing to compare you to nor to reason you by, and therefore they instinctively abuse what they don't understand. This does not mean that you should settle for a life of abuse and neglect. Low esteem is not of God. However, we often place too much of a premium on the importance of acceptance when considering where we are planted. Then, when we are offended, we uproot ourselves and transplant to other places based upon our self-determined criteria of stability. As the seed, you should look to your planter as the source of all things. When you are planted by God, He alone is the author and finisher of your faith, your provider, and the one responsible for validating all emotional needs.

He planted you where you are strategically and purposefully. It was not so that you could rest on your laurels and skate through this experience called life. Instead, there is a side of God or a revelation of Him that is missing in your particular family, neighborhood, job, region, or nation. So, since you realize that you *are* the blessing, and that you are resourceful, you must now replicate the Kingdom revelation that lies within you, and do so until this concept fills your given environment.

Replication is repeating the process of production. The K-Gene equips you to be productive, resourceful, and to produce something that is beneficial to your environment. Replication is re-engineering that process in order to mass produce that item, concept, merchandise, etc. Production is important because it gives you something of substance that can be beneficial to the environment. However, productivity does not denote mastery of that process. Inventors would attest to the fact that some of their greatest inventions were birthed from trial and error. It took numerous attempts to get to the desired goal, most of these leading to failure. Once success has been attained, however, if no notes were taken, then the victory is short-lived. It's one thing to engineer a product; it is quite another to master it. In your resourcefulness, have you captured and mastered the process that brought you to your fruitful state? If not, then you are unable to repeat the successful process and multiply it according to God's intention. You were not meant to go through life making it from process to process. You are wired to master the process, taking dominion over your environment by making everything bend toward God's revelation through you.

This is the power of replication. It allows you to capture the correct methodology to ensure that you can repeat these authentic accomplishments. There is power in your experiences because the knowledge that you gained has the potential to equip you with sustained victory. How many lessons did you conquer during your desert season? The keys you earned during this rough patch will be useful in maintaining your newfound resourcefulness.

As a set of Kingdom principles, replication and replenishment work hand in hand toward God's desired end for dominion. God is glorified when the knowledge of Him fills your environment. He is not simply interested in Kingdom knowledge being present in places of your personal realm — it must dominate the atmosphere, filling every space and overtaking all

opposing ideologies. This was God's intention when
He first articulated replication and replenishment.
According to Genesis 1:28, God instructs man to first
be fruitful. He then commands humanity to multiply
(replicate) and then to replenish the earth. While God
was talking about filling the earth with more humanity,
this was not the totality of God's will. As His Kingdom
ambassadors on earth, God wants us to replenish the
earth with His thoughts, His ways, His level of living
and reigning. In fact, the word "replenish" actually
means to make complete and fill. We serve an awesome
God who could have both created and filled the earth
Himself. However, in His pursuit to have fellowship
with His most prized creations, He provided Adam a
reasonable start and then partnered with this man to
complete the work. He (God) created the animals and
gave them the ability to reproduce. He created the
oceans and the vast lands and then left all of this under

man's care with the instructions to replenish the earth. God's decision to partner with mankind continued even after the fall in the Garden, and it remains to this day. He is just that into us that He would reserve part of His work to be done in tandem with humanity.

Remember, God plants us in the place where there is a deficiency of the Kingdom truth that He wishes to reveal through us. Therefore, once He has planted you, God expects you to replicate His revelation and replenish (fill) your environment with that knowledge until it becomes the manifested reality. As a planted seed, this means that your season is fulfilled when people around you have had the chance to accept or actively reject the knowledge of God that you carry. Authentic replication requires a mastery of the process. One cannot master this process without intimacy, without a close experiential working knowledge base.

You carry a unique and special revelation of God's Kingdom within you. This is the reason why you are planted where you are. You are responsible for promoting this vision to the point that it becomes a sweet and enticing savor to those around you. However, before it can be of true benefit to those around you, it must first affect you. Salesmen understand the power of testing the value of their product. You are more convincing when your product becomes part of your personal narrative as opposed to a secondhand account. As the carrier of God's vision, you should be the first partaker. Are you personally aware of the power of the vision you carry? Do you know its value and worth? How does the Kingdom system that you carry operate? Without practical knowledge of your vision, you will be unable to gain mastery. Without mastery, there can be no replication. No replication means no ability to replenish your realm. When we don't replenish our realms, it leads to a prolonged season in the place where you were planted. If you find yourself dissatisfied with your surroundings, it may help to assess whether you have allowed God to properly plant you in His will. Only then can you begin to replicate and replenish the atmosphere where you've been sown. Only then will you be found mature enough to gain access to the inheritance that God designed for you.

NOTES OF REFLECTION

IMPLEMENTING THE K-GENE

CHAPTER 8: WHAT'S YOUR FUNCTION?

The Kingdom is made up of many sons of God. You are not the only son. In fact, the beauty of Christ's sacrifice was that one Son was sowed as a seed into the earth to produce many sons of God. Likewise there are many gifts, but there is only one calling. This fact makes sense as the Bible also makes clear that there are many members, but only one body. The many members of the body thus all share the same calling. Furthermore, The Bible states that there is one hope that belongs to the calling that we have collectively received (Ephesians 4:4). Many callings in one body would result in a disjointed and divided system, so it is best to think of the many members functioning together in harmony to fulfill one major goal. So what is our calling under Kingdom? What is the collective goal that we are to work together to promote? This calling is to the ministry of reconciliation.

In order for us to have "received" the ministry of reconciliation, it had to be given by God. The word "gave," which comes from the Greek word *didomi*, means to give, to bestow, to bring forth, or to commit. Essentially, God committed or entrusted to the entire Kingdom the ministry of reconciliation. Some people mistake this type of giving with the connotation of a gift. The faulty viewpoint here, however, is that such an outlook removes us from the burden of responsibility that is associated with a calling rather than a gift. A gift, when given, has no strings attached or expectations assigned to it. Think of a gift you give someone for Christmas or for their birthday; it is given with the freedom and liberty for the beneficiary to use that gift in whatever way they see fit. There are no strong associations with the giver's intent and the receiver's use. However, think about entrusting your child into the hands of another person. This is not a gift, as you will surely be returning to collect your child eventually. Therefore, there are expectations and standards that you mandate to be upheld in anticipation of your return. In fact, you want your child to be in the same if not a better condition than when you left them. God's ministry of reconciliation is the same. It is a trusteeship, or better yet, a stewardship. God committed and entrusted this ministry of reconciliation to us all and He will require its progress at the hand of the collective body of Christ.

As I stated in chapter 3, I believe that the ministry of reconciliation entails two parts: (1) salvation and (2) sonship. When these components are brought together reconciliation is the ability to bring restoration to the broken *fellowship* between God and man, and to restore humanity to our proper status enjoyed in Eden. Notice that the operative word here is "fellowship" and not

"relationship." The account in Genesis of the creation

of man proves that all humanity is related to God. He

made us in His image and in His likeness. However, the

concepts of relationship and fellowship are different.

There are plenty of children who are related to fathers

that they may never know. They carry their father's

DNA inside of them, but unfortunately would not be

able to pick them out in a police lineup. Without

fellowship, the relationship is meaningless and fruitless.

No inheritance is secure when there is only

relationship. Fellowship is indicative of trust and

intimacy, which takes time. In fact, power and riches

can only be properly delineated through the channel of

fellowship. You would not entrust your most priceless

possessions to a stranger with whom you had no

rapport or trust. People who only embrace the system of

church are satisfied with mere relationship, but

Kingdom people are not satisfied until they have fellowship. They seek God's undivided attention, and they hold no secrets from Him. Eventually, barriers are destroyed in fellowship because both parties willingly move away facades, fears, and pretenses.

Reconciliation is something that was initiated from above ("reconciliation" in the New Testament is often based on the Greek word *kata*, which means "downward"). God initiated the process of reconciliation by sending His Son, Jesus Christ, into the earth to be the propitiation or atonement for our sins. Remember, Jesus' message was for us to repent, for the Kingdom of Heaven is at hand. He preaches the message of Kingdom, which is the complete message of reconciliation.

What's interesting about our call is that the one who is called must commit all that they are for the sake of the end goal. We easily praise the effective work of

Jesus Christ's bloodshed on the cross without

considering the fact that we must also bear the cross

ourselves. Whether it is rebuilding race relations,

negotiating peace between nation-states, or brokering

relations among broken family members, reconciliation

is a messy and often-times bloody process. We live in a

politically correct society that seeks to sweep things

under the proverbial rug without ever genuinely

wrestling with issues to come to true solutions. True

peace is not found by ignoring problems, but in finding

holistic approaches that fully remedy every aspect of

life. Reconciliation calls for both sides to step away

from their respective end zones, closer to the 50-yard

line. As James eloquently writes of the Father's heart,

"draw near unto God and He will draw near you."

However, even here we must highlight the fact that in

our reconciliation to God He went further than 50

percent and He gave His all, by giving us His only Son, Jesus Christ.

This example serves not only as an awe-inspiring moment in history, but also as a model of how the believer should approach reconciliation. Whereas it would be ideal to only have to give 50 percent toward the cause of reconciliation, Kingdom citizens understand the mandate to bridge the gap, no matter what the distance is. This is what Jesus was referring to when He stated that anyone who wanted to enter the level of discipleship must "take up their cross and follow me." Here, the word "cross" is symbolic of death or extenuating sacrifice. Because the Kingdom is called to the ministry of reconciliation, we must be prepared to give excessively, liberally, and frequently. This type of giving may be more than what those who need to be reconciled will give, but it is necessary all the same. Does this mean we are to be the saviors of the world? Not at all, for there was already one Savior, Jesus Christ, who purchased the salvation of all people by dying on the cross. However, reconciliation will cause us to sacrifice our time; our talents; our resources; our reputations; and, for some of us, our very lives.

So, we have figured out that we all share the same collective calling. It is the Kingdom mandate that burdens every believer to serve as ministers of reconciliation. While we all share the same calling, the body of Christ is filled with a diversity of gifts. Each one of us is uniquely gifted in one or more areas of life. We are good dancers, writers, athletes, singers, chefs, financiers, etc. While there are a diversity of gifts, they are all made to be complementary to every other gift. That's right — no one gift can show the full picture of Christ or express the full capability of Kingdom. We need every gift operating together, and at full capacity,

to help broaden the reach of reconciliation.

Consider the analogy of Georgetown Cupcakes. I

frequently visit this place, which became famous for its

TV show, *D.C. Cupcakes*. When I go to Georgetown

Cupcakes, I go with the goal of purchasing and eating

cupcakes. It is my responsibility to provide the money

in exchange for this service that they are providing.

Once the money is supplied, it is the collective

responsibility of D.C. Cupcakes to deliver the product.

However, everyone will play a different role in

fulfilling that overarching goal. The cashiers are at the

frontlines, receiving the money, and taking down the

orders of the customers. The quantity and identity of

the cupcakes are relayed to the kitchen staff. In the

kitchen, there are those who are gifted in making and

processing the batter for each specific cupcake. Then,

there are those who are skilled in baking the cupcakes

and icing them, to make them both delectable and appealing to the eye. Finally, the cupcakes are sent to the front of the store to be packaged in boxes uniquely designed with the logo and color of the D.C. Cupcake brand. It will be these packagers that will present to me the product that I paid for, however, every department functioned in sync with one another to fulfill the major calling of providing me with a cupcake.

This same system of operation holds true for the Kingdom. We have one calling, but different roles to play within it. So the better question is not "what are you called to do?" but actually "what is your function?" What role do you play in the Kingdom call of reconciliation? What is your part in fulfilling the ultimate mandate that is on the body of Christ to reconcile humanity back to fellowship with God?

When God commissioned Moses to return to Egypt to advocate for the deliverance of the Israelites, Moses began to voice his concerns to God. Moses understood

his mission, but his problem was understanding *how* he

would achieve success. What tool would he use to

accomplish God's will? How would he function? God

responded by asking a simple question: What is that in

your hand?" (Exodus 4:2 KJV). God is omniscient,

which means that He knows everything. Therefore,

when He posed this question, He already knew Moses'

strengths and weaknesses. God understood Moses'

apprehension, and even knew the outcome of the

mission that He had assigned to the former prince of

Egypt. In asking this question, God was really requiring

Moses to assess his surroundings and capabilities. He

wanted Moses to figure out his functionality. Often,

after we have realized that we have a purpose, God

prompts us to seek out our functionality. What are your

strengths? What are you good at? What tools have you

already been given to help you carry out the mandate as

ministers of reconciliation? You must figure out your functionality so that you can determine what your Kingdom contribution is to God's plan. You have something to offer God, and this world. Something that sets you apart from every other person, yet complementary to every other gift out there. Like Moses' rod, your gift may seem inadequate to you. It may make you feel vulnerable and thus, like Moses, you don't like to exercise this functionality because it is uncomfortable. However, it is still the gift that God has given you to affect His world. The sooner you find your functionality, the quicker you will be able to find the place where you fit in. This body is for you, and this inheritance is yours for the taking, once you fulfill your functionality.

NOTES OF REFLECTION

CHAPTER 9: CAN YOU STAND TO BE TRAINED?

All sons are heirs to the inheritances of their fathers. The mark of a good father is that he leaves an inheritance to his children and grandchildren. Eventually, these sons will have access to the same money, power, influence, and land that the patriarch amassed. However, that access is usually only granted to heirs that show that they are mature enough to handle the responsibility that comes along with such authority. Maturity is the key to all the inheritance God has for you.

When kings are looking to the future of their kingdoms, they begin assessing their lineage to see who has the ability to carry on the legacy. Reigning over a realm or kingdom is not a light matter, and requires balanced and steady leadership. Every decision made by the leader directly impacts each individual connected to their realm. It can be quite devastating when an immature heir sits on the throne of power; their inability to lead a people often causes civil unrest. In these cases, the story either ends with a dictatorship rife with governmental violations and abuses or revolutions by the citizenry that overthrow the leadership. At least this is the case with earthly leadership.

God's Kingdom is slightly different in this respect. God is an eternal being. He is a spirit. Remember, when we die our flesh will cease to exist, while our spirits will live on. Thus, as a spirit, God's life will never end and neither will his reign. His Kingdom truly is established for all eternity. Therefore, when we speak of legacy and heirs in God's Kingdom, we are talking about reigning together under God. He will always be

King, and none of us will ever take His throne. No force will ever overtake our God, or usurp His authority --- Consider Lucifer's fate when he attempted to do so. God has designed His Kingdom in a way that allows us the opportunity to serve as regents in the earth in His stead. Think of the roles of ambassadors in foreign countries. They are the representatives of the presidents or monarchs who appoint them. They are afforded the same weight, rights, and credibility as the leader who gave them the commission. As ambassadors of Christ, the K-Gene is your inheritance and it qualifies you to reign in the earth in the same manner your King reigns in Heaven. When there is immature leadership in God's Kingdom, it becomes a poor reflection of God in the earth. When we refuse to walk in excellence, or when we reject the call to holy living, we mute the expression of the K-Gene and cover up the true, unvarnished image of God within us. Such individuals are the heirs that God is unable to trust with the full weight of His intended inheritance for them.

Mature leadership is effective leadership because it provides maximum benefits for all parties concerned. Outside of Adam, Eve, and Christ, no heir has ever been born mature. In God's Kingdom, we are works in progress in need of training and cultivation. The K-Gene within you comes complete with the same leadership style as the God who formed you. Yet without proper conditioning, this Gene will never express itself and will be reduced to untapped potential. So the question of leadership is not one of infallibility but rather of endurance. When God is looking for heirs to represent Him in this earth, He is not looking for those who are faultless, but for those who can stand to be trained. Can you stand to be trained? Can you, with all of your gifts and abilities, humble yourself? Are you willing to endure this process, so that the K-Gene can be on display unfiltered?

As heirs, when our mindset is one of entitlement, as if we are *owed* the wealth or we have earned it somehow, we end up squandering the fortune that we are given. Remember, a good man leaves an inheritance to his children's children … which means the wealth that is given to you by your father is not really to be spent, but to be stewarded and invested to create a return for the generation that follows you. In turn, you will leave an inheritance that is for your grandchildren, but your children will be its stewards. This is how legacies are maintained and preserved.

The more I look at the story of the prodigal son, the more I am convinced that it reinforces this principle of the mature heir. Let's forget the older son who was bitter in his servitude to their father. Set aside the work that the father had done to help secure an inheritance for his two sons. In fact, let's set aside the cultural and paternal disrespect that the youngest shows in seeking the inheritance while the father lived. After all, Jesus was presenting to us a parable regarding the length and depth of God's loving ability to overcome our sins and inadequacy. Instead, we will simply focus on the prodigal son and his request for his inheritance.

Had this been a story about real situations, there is a good chance that the younger son had worked hard over the years, in service to his father. He helped his father and brother maintain the land, the servants, and all the rest of the father's property. The fact that his father released allotments unto both sons was a sign that there was an inheritance that was stored up for them. The youngest son asked for his inheritance and the father gave each of his sons their due portion. Upon receiving his share of his heritage, the youngest son immediately departed and wasted all of his wealth on things that were counter to his well-being. Whether or not he had a right to ask for his inheritance, his biggest problem was his attitude about its purpose. Remember, any worthwhile patriarch leaves an inheritance to his grandchildren, so in reality it wasn't within the son's right to spend all of his heritage. The wealth transfer that he received wasn't for him alone, but was meant to be sustained until at least the next generation. As an heir to God's Kingdom, you also must be careful that you don't squander all the wealth on yourself. The transfer of power, authority, and prosperity is meant to outlast you and carry on to the next generation. This doesn't mean that you should not utilize portions of your birthright — after all you will need it to live. However, you should seek to maximize your wealth for future generations by making investments instead of wasteful spending.

Heirs who are mature think in terms of investments and returns that best benefit future generations. Being a steward of God's Kingdom calls for discarding selfish mentalities, and being willing sustain God's legacy for future generations of Kingdom agents. When heirs adopt this mentality they show that they have earned God's trust and can now access their rightful inheritance.

It is the responsibility of the king to train his heirs, and the job of fathers to train their sons. The patriarch must bring the heirs to the place where they can receive, maintain, and then multiply the inheritance that they have been given. Immature heirs stand the chance of wasting God's Kingdom resources, and thus serving as ineffective ambassadors for His Kingdom. God therefore has a vested interest in ensuring that we, as heirs of His promises, are trained and cultivated to handle the responsibilities that come from our spiritual lineage. When God invests Himself in us (whether it be an investment of His power, authority, resources, etc.), there is an expectation that we will maintain these resources and then amplify their usefulness in the earth. Mature heirs have the ability to take every investment and give God a great return. Though all humanity is endowed with the K-Gene, it takes training and development to awaken the Gene's potential and bring us to the place of capable inheritors. When God is ready to develop us from childhood to mature heirs, He will often utilize the processes of life to help conform us into the image of Christ. That boss that gets on your nerves, bankruptcy, eviction notices; health crises … God allows these events to take place in our lives to bring us to the place of Kingdom submission and realignment with His will. Remember, God's ultimate goal is to reconcile us with our original status of dominion with Him. Prior to sin entering in the world,

Adam and Eve were formed as mature heirs. At creation, God immediately endued us with power and authority to be stewards over His handiwork on earth. There was no development needed, no growth necessary. Man was genetically predisposed to be in proper alignment with His Creator. After man's rebellion, disobedience and wickedness reigned in our mortal bodies, yet God's inheritance was still open to us. All humanity thus moved from being mature heirs to living below our rightful means. With the K-Gene lying dormant within us, we pursued the desires of our flesh and built the products of our God-deprived mind. Before sin, man had only one commandment: "Do not eat of the tree of knowledge of good and evil." Humanity was a mature heir and there was no need for excessive handholding.

Heirs who are ripe for the promise execute wise judgment and discretion with limited accountability.

They have developed internal convictions and natural tendencies that are in line with their responsibilities. In Kingdom, these would be the people who love the Lord with all of our heart, mind, and soul. Out of that love, such people lead consistently yielded lives of surrender to God through Christ. For these people, alignment with God has become a natural tendency. They have learned to hold an appetite for the things God desires and likewise to reject what He detests. These mature Kingdom inheritors don't live right because of fear of God's punishment; they do not rely on the ethical codes of accountability that pastors and Christian colleagues often provide. Whether they are being watched or are alone, they are regulated by an internal desire to simply please the Lord.

After Adam and Eve's transgression, immaturity was our default position. And therefore, God had to find a process to train us to adequately access our

Kingdom inheritance. We suddenly saw a

multiplication of God's commandments from one

(under Adam) to the Ten Commandments (under

Moses). These commandments, known as the law,

provided a standard and code for man to follow in

hopes that the law would help humanity mature into

their inheritances. This is the principle that Paul

outlines in Galatians 4:1-2. "Now I say, That the heir,

as longs as he is a child differeth nothing from a

servant, though he be lord of all; But is under tutors and

governors until the appointed time of the father" (KJV).

Notice that the heir is lord of all. He is bequeathed all

the riches and wealth that his father intended, however,

his access is denied as long as this heir is a child. As

long as he reasons and responds in an inadequate or

immature way, he is ineligible to access his promise.

According to Paul's principle, when an heir responds in

immature ways, he is put under the watchful care of

tutors and governors. In other words, the heir is assigned taskmasters to help cultivate him into a mature heir who can responsibly exercise control over his environment. Whether it was the Mosaic law of Old Testament times or today's hardships, these governors and tutors were never meant to crush us but to bring us into alignment with Kingdom. God knows our individual strengths and weaknesses. He knows the thorns in our sides and all of our vulnerabilities. He utilizes the trials of life to strengthen our submission to Him. In actuality, that annoying boss, that untimely eviction notice, that bankruptcy might just be there to assess whether you are a child or a mature heir ready to walk into your destiny. If it seems like you are in a season where all your pressure points are being stressed, this may be God's gracious way of maturing you for something greater, your inheritance in Him.

So again, the question is this: "Can you stand to be trained?" You must switch your mentality to see life's obstacles as the perfect training ground for your growth and development. The K-Gene within you makes you predisposed to victory, thus you were designed to overcome and survive life's temporary trials. It is time that you identify your governors and tutors and yield to their purpose in your life. Doing so will give you access to the fulfilled destiny that you earnestly desire.

NOTES OF REFLECTION

CHAPTER 10: THE ART OF WAR

Anybody remember the classic board game Monopoly? I was obsessed with this game as a child. It was a game that called for patience, strategy, and instincts. It was also a game of discipline. The premise was simple yet instructive at the same time: each player was given a symbolic token that served as their representative within the game. The square board was a mixture of properties, varying in value, public utilities, railroads, and a jailhouse. All players were apportioned the same amount of initial capital, with one player serving as the banker. There was a total of $15,140 allotted to the bank. As the name of the game implies, the goal was for one player to use the limited number of dollars and limited resources to create a monopoly of the board. This game fascinated me because it was empire-building at its best, and called for each player to strategically employ soft and hard power tactics to win. It wasn't until later in life that I would realize the bigger lesson that Monopoly taught me — the importance of possessing territory.

Territory has been the catalyst behind numerous wars and conflicts in human history. Every person earnestly desires a plot of land that they can call their own. Nations, too, determine their identity and worth by the size of their territory. Consider the age-old Israeli-Palestinian conflict. They have been fighting over 2,402 square miles of territory for millennia. Both sides understand the links between land acquisition, identity, and the right to self-determination. Disregarding boundaries could ignite a conflict instantaneously, due to the perception of an impending conquest.

Yes, there is absolute value in territory. In fact, one of the key attributes of any kingdom or nation is its possession of territory. A nation cannot exist without land, a kingdom cannot exist without territory. And, similar to Monopoly, we are all in a quest for the biggest portions that we can attain.

I have purposely used the term "territory" more than "land," because land is a component of territory. Territory is any space that is set aside for ownership. This can include land, airspace, and even spiritual realms. There are physical kingdoms and invisible kingdoms, each with different identities and purposes. However, all kingdoms share one common characteristic, an insatiable appetite for expansion. We want more until there is nothing left to conquer, and we will accomplish this by any means necessary.

We have established that every kingdom has territory, and that all kingdoms seek to expand their influence, power, and boundaries. Therefore, any kingdom seeking to endure must raise up an army. These armies are most often composed of citizens of the kingdom or nation-state. They have a vested interest in protecting the lives and rights of their family, friends, and fellow countrymen. Building a sizeable army can often serve as a deterring force to outsiders seeking vulnerable prey. Yet an army's biggest benefit comes in defending the homeland in times of war. War is an inevitable part of life, and people should be prepared for these eventualities.

Sons of God are citizens of His Kingdom, and thus eligible to be enlisted in His army. The ultimate dictate of this army is to secure the territory that has been gained and seek every opportunity to expand and advance Kingdom's influence. While many earthly kingdoms define territory and influence in terms of land, the Kingdom of Heaven views territory in terms of the number of hearts and minds that willingly submit to God through Jesus Christ. There are two main kingdoms that measure territorial gain by the number of hearts and minds that yield to its mandates: the Kingdom of Heaven and the kingdom of darkness. Like Monopoly, there are fixed and limiting conditions that are placed upon both of these kingdoms: time and capacity. In terms of time, this battle of wits between the two kingdoms will end after Christ has subdued all things for the Kingdom of God. Capacity will be fulfilled when all mankind has had the opportunity to choose an allegiance to one of the two kingdoms. The precise outcomes of these things is only known by God. When we, as earthly vessels, yield ourselves to God's influence then Kingdom is translated before us and manifested among us.

This was the sense of submission that Christ pointed us toward when He taught His disciples to pray

"Thy Kingdom come thy will be done on earth, as it is in Heaven." Earth was built to follow Heaven's lead; mankind was built with the ultimate intent that we willingly defer our rights to the King of Heaven. When sinners come to trust in the redeeming power of Jesus Christ, Kingdom territory is expanded. When the hearts and minds of people are reconciled back to the Father, Kingdom territory grows larger. The kingdom of darkness, seeking its own pursuits, attempts to subvert these efforts and expand its own territory. The hearts and minds that openly reject God's Kingdom way are the terrain of the kingdom of darkness. When we choose to yield to the works of the flesh, we are expanding the territory of the kingdom of darkness. As you can now see plainly, there is a war going on, and it is imperative that gained territory be protected and expanded territory be pursued. As soldiers of the Kingdom of Heaven, it is important that we fight for

Kingdom expansion. As carriers of the K-Gene, we have an essential, vested interest in protecting and expanding our gains. After all, if this Kingdom were to cease to exist (which is impossible), so would the relevance of the K-gene within us, and the inheritance that we seek. However, while it is important that we fight, we must also make war correctly. We must understand the art of war, the principles that make soldiers efficient, and the tools needed to achieve victory. In essence, we will discuss *how* we fight.

Soldiers must have a mission.

All wars must have goals, metrics, and benchmarks. Without any of these things, military conflicts become unorganized campaigns with no winners and no end in sight. When engaging in war, it is the responsibility of the king or commander in chief to provide the metrics, boundaries, resources, and scope of the mission.

Soldiers must accept a mission that is in line with the expressed will of the ruler. Christ's overall mission has been to reconcile us with the Father. In the context of *The K-Gene*, reconciliation is the two-fold process of salvation and sonship. Therefore, the mission for all soldiers should be to promote and defend this brand of reconciliation.

Missions are important because they provide soldiers with clarity and organization. They often define one clear problem, one enemy, and the potential pathway to win the fight. As ministers of reconciliation, we war against the kingdom of darkness to defend the hearts and minds that have been turned to God. This is an honorable and valuable mission. Truly, this is a war campaign for the priceless souls of humanity. Once the mission has been outlined and expressed, it is the responsibility of each soldier to ensure that they are aware of the mission.

In accepting their commissions, they choose to support the overall mission whether or not they personally agree with or understand every detail. You are a soldier in the Lord's army, and you have a mission that He has specifically given you. Your mission fits perfectly with the united mission of winning and maintaining territory for the Kingdom of God. What did He call you to do? What is your purpose as a soldier? How do you defend the territory that belongs to Kingdom? Because we are carriers of the K-Gene, we should have the same appetite for the things that God desires — we should have a desire to fulfill the mission that we have been given. This was the type of appetite that Jesus referred to when He declared, "My meat is to do the will of Him that sent me." Jesus was saying that He received sustenance and satisfaction from carrying out God's mandate. As Kingdom citizens, we get our fulfillment from serving our King, and that includes fulfilling the missions that He outlines.

Soldiers must be focused.

After soldiers have been given a mission, they must focus all their energy on completing that task. There is no room for error or distractions, as either could jeopardize the lives of those around you, and slow the progress of the mission. Being a soldier calls for a high level of discipline and restraint.

Times of war are times of great sacrifice for service members. The higher the stakes, the greater the sacrifice. This is one reason why many armies have stringent training and selection processes — military leadership wants to determine whether someone has the stamina, drive, and discipline to last in turmoil and conflict. From ancient Greece to the present day, there has been a pact between governments and their armies to ensure that all of the standard needs of the soldiers are well taken care of. This is a necessary measure to ensure that soldiers are not encumbered with life's challenges while they fight on the battlefield. The Apostle Paul instructs his mentee, Timothy, in this very same principle, when speaking of Christian warfare. "No man that warreth entangleth himself with the affairs of this life that he may please him who hath chosen him to be a soldier" (2 Timothy 2:4 KJV).

I have never been to war, however, I do know that it involves strategy, endurance, patience, and adequate manpower. Many wars are campaigns that last months or even years, and in hostile environments a soldier who is distracted by other things risks being killed in action. Unfortunately, this distracted state is how some of us live. We engage in life's battlefield with our minds on numerous questions that are really beyond our control, questions like What will I eat?, Where will I live?, What will I wear?" Meanwhile the keys to your spiritual success pass you by, and you become prone to attacks from the enemy. The truth is that God has already supplied our needs so that we can be free to focus on the important work of gaining territory for Kingdom.

Look back at earlier seasons of your life and consider how often chaos and distractions showed up right after you received instruction from God. Remember how crystal clear it was when God shared His vision for you? It was an idea, a seed kernel from God that was meant to attract the hearts and minds of men toward a Kingdom lifestyle. Recall how sure you were of what you heard, and how to go about carrying it out. This time of serenity was when God embedded His will in simple terms, so that there would be no confusion. It wasn't until you got up from this time of prayer and attempted to move forward in life that all the chaos and busyness ensued. Suddenly, you were reminded of all the bills that you had; there were demands on your time, your mind, and your strength. You quickly found yourself feeling overwhelmed, and God's mission was the last thing on your mind.

This is the main tactic that the enemy uses to draw our focus away from our mission and toward the pursuit for material things. The K-Gene is your connection to God's way, and it triggers the hunger in you for Kingdom expansion. Supporting this hunger and maintaining this focus should be a priority. Therefore, when the enemy attacks our resolve and sways us from God's clear path, we should reset our minds. Jesus taught His disciples to seek Kingdom first, and allow all other sources to follow. When we maintain our focus on Kingdom, we become the fit and qualified soldiers that God built us to be.

Soldiers must know their enemy.

There is a danger in underestimating your enemy, devaluing the competition, and taking their influence lightly. Many people who make this mistake do so because they don't really know their enemy. They don't understand how their adversary functions and operates. I wonder what your response would be if I asked you to identify your enemy and describe their methodology. Do you know your enemy? Do you understand their patterns and the system they operate in? If the answer to these questions is "No," then you should take the time to understand your opponent. You can't build an effective strategy to win a war if you don't study your enemy.

"Haters" has become the buzzword of the decade, especially in some of our Pentecostal churches. It has become the code language that we use to describe those who don't agree with the decisions we make, or people who won't take the time to acknowledge our potential

and "greatness." While these elements do exist in life,

and some people act like haters, I fear that we have

built a culture that has taken these same people and

painted them to be the enemy. We give haters a lot of

real estate in our minds, a lot of time in our sermons

(because it preaches well), and we take that bitterness

and use it to identify *people* as our enemies. We do this

with mere mortals, flesh and blood like us, despite the

fact that the Bible clearly outlines that we don't wrestle

with flesh and blood. In essence, we have mistaken the

identity of our enemy.

Your enemy is very real, he does exist, and you

know him as Satan. However, this enemy is an enemy

of yours because he is God's enemy. Satan is opposed

to God and all the things that God has designed. As

carriers of the K-Gene, made in the image and likeness

of God, the devil can't stand you. Your mere existence

is a witness to the power and sovereignty of God, and this offends Satan, bruising his prideful ego. Your enemy is not your annoying boss, your scheming neighbor, or your family member who you can't stand right now. No, in fact your enemy could never be flesh — the forces of Satan utilize willing, fleshly vessels, but the core of your problem is not natural, but spiritual. Remember, God is a spirit, you are a spiritual being, and therefore your enemy is also spiritual in nature. As Ephesians 6:12 reminds us, "We wrestle against principalities, powers, the rulers of the darkness of this world, and spiritual wickedness in high places" (KJV).

All of these factions are spiritual, forces that cannot be seen, yet they exert their influence in the earth. Their existence predates the existence of humanity, and they have been enemies of God since before the concept of chronological time. So, your enemies are the forces that make up the kingdom of darkness, not people, but spiritual forces. They are your enemies because they are opposed to God, our King, whom we serve. Remember, this K-Gene is the genetic trace of our Father, and a threat to God is a threat to us.

So how does the enemy operate? What is his methodology? When we look in Genesis, the first time we see Satan is in the Garden of Eden. He is in the form of a serpent, and described as subtle. He is very covert, hardly seen either physically or in his methodology. He sits in the background and attempts to manipulate situations without ever really being credited as the author of the schemes and traps that he sets. He doesn't need credit, and I would dare to say that he is not seeking credit. He is, however, seeking your demise, and wants to wipe you off of this earth. As his tactic was in the Garden, it remains the same today. The enemy relies on the powers of coercion and persuasion.

Let's be clear, the enemy doesn't jump in our bodies and make us do anything without permission. The excuse "I couldn't help myself" will not hold up in the court of God because we all have the ability to choose, yet the persuasive powers of the enemy should never be underestimated.

As Paul told us in Ephesians, our adversaries are principalities. Principalities are ruling forces, and the word "principles" is a derivative of the same source word. A principle is a foundational thought or belief that a system is built upon. Therefore, it would stand to reason that the enemy uses words and thoughts to attack us. In the Garden, Satan never forced Eve to take the fruit; he reasoned with her until she rationalized within herself that what she would gain was worth more than her obedience to God. This is the same primary tool that the enemy uses against us today. He waits until God releases a word, and then he counters that Word with an opposing thought. This then makes

you choose between the uncomfortable course that God

is requiring versus the convenient pathway that Satan

offers. Soldiers who know this enemy know how to

counteract his attacks. They expect to be confronted

once they have heard from God, and they preempt the

enemy by filling their minds and hearts with God's

Word. Knowing your enemy can help you avoid

Satan's traps and pitfalls that are meant to delay you

from reaching your destiny.

Soldiers know how to use the proper weaponry.

Have you ever heard the phrase, "Never bring a knife to

a gunfight"? The person with the knife is at a clear

disadvantage unless they are highly trained to dodge

bullets, while getting close enough to strike their

opponent. Soldiers who aren't familiar with weaponry,

and the proper tool that fits the fight, stand the chance

of bringing weapons that are inadequate for the conflict. In order to win, our weaponry must possess power that is either equal to or greater than the arsenal of the enemy. God is Sovereign, and because He reigns over all, everything He has is superior to anything that could be made or imagined. We have discovered that our adversary uses the power of persuasion to get us to buy into systems that are counter Kingdom. We must fight this enemy and resist his assaults at all costs, as soldiers in the army of God. Therefore, we must know our weaponry, and it's intended effect and purpose.

In 2 Corinthians 10, Paul is in the process of vindicating himself and his apostolic calling. Given his past, prior to becoming the Christian giant who we now revere, it is quite possible that Paul struggled with his own thoughts on his qualifications. Paul may have been engaged in a mind-battle with the enemy. You understand how relentless the enemy can be. You walk through this life fighting urges of your former life and instincts to go back to a comfortable place. You go to sleep sometimes as a mechanism to silence the constant bombardment of thoughts that the enemy throws your way. The only problem is, when you wake up those thoughts are still lodged in your thoughts and they ruin your day from start to finish. How do you fight against this constant pressure to disobey God? Paul comes to the conclusion that we war in spiritual terms, and thus require spiritual weaponry. The effect of our weaponry must be strong enough to overthrow these thoughts that we struggle with.

"For the weapons of our warfare are not carnal, but mighty through God to the pulling down of strongholds; Casting down imaginations and every high thing that exalteth itself against the knowledge of God, and bringing every thought to the obedience of Christ"

(2 Corinthians 10:4–5 KJV).

Our weapons are spiritual in nature, and they are indeed strong enough to cast down the thoughts, systems, and principalities that come against us. The task is to make sure every thought that passes through our minds eventually conforms to the will of Christ or is evicted. Because we underestimate our enemy and don't know the weapons that we have, many of us simply settle for the thoughts that pass through our minds. We feel hopeless and paralyzed by the foundational thoughts that are presented to us and we adopt a tone of silence and submission. Yet there is a K-Gene inside of you that makes you feel uneasy every time you attempt to settle into this slumber of defeat. You feel uncomfortable because everything in your spiritual

DNA is structured for dominion and authority, thus passivity never sits well with you.

Do you know the specific weapons in your arsenal that help you fight against the ploys of the enemy? They are tools that you heard of, even if you are unaware that they are your weapons. I'm talking about the powerful weaponry of prayer, Scripture reading, faith, and obedience. Wrapped up all in one, these components strengthen you to use your power of choice in a way that reflects the Kingdom desires that lie in you. Remember, it was the misinformed choice of Adam and Eve that caused us to lose the battle in Eden, so it will take Kingdom-informed choices to win the war of souls. The end goal of the warfare is to get people to choose one of the two major spiritual kingdoms. You are only as strong as your activated K-Gene. Therefore it is imperative that you combat every contrary thought by reading God's Word and meditating on it.

Do you recall that old Sunday school song, "Read your Bible, pray every day, then you'll grow, grow, grow"? Who would have known that, as a child, you were being equipped with the strategy to overcome obstacles beyond your years and capacity? We read God's Word because it informs our thinking and it nourishes us. God's Word literally places God thoughts within us, giving us the mental capacity to withstand the mind games of the enemy. Too often, we neglect to read our Bible because we don't properly understand its importance. We should not read the Word because we fear repercussion from God if we neglect our devotion. We read because doing so restores us to soundness of mind in God, and allows us to live obedient lives patterned after Kingdom.

When we read the Word daily, it gives us something to meditate on, and fuels our prayer life. To meditate literally means "to mutter to oneself." It is not just the action of thinking about something, but rehearsing it verbally until it becomes your reality. The prize for meditation is stability, or the ability to withstand every season and all of Satan's attacks while still bearing fruit consistently. Don't let the enemy steal your voice! Meditate day and night, as Psalm 1 suggests. Doing this serves as a weapon of vigilance at all hours of the day, to protect you from the fiery thoughts of the enemy.

Prayers during times of warfare are different from petitioning prayers. Petitions are the types of prayer that most of us identify with. These are the prayers where you bring God your list of requests, desires, and needs. Your objective is to see God move in the areas where you personally need Him. Petitioning prayers sometimes lack surety and confidence because we don't always know the will of God, and what He intends to do. Will He answer my petition exactly as I asked? Is this a situation where He denies my request, in order to teach me a bigger lesson? These are examples of the questions that we hold in our psyche when we pray petitioning prayers.

Warfare prayers are more direct and emboldened. Kingdom soldiers who have been given their mission understand the mind of God concerning that particular task. Therefore, these prayers are filled with commands that are sanctioned by God. These prayers literally have the weight and force of the God whom we serve. If you are reading your Bible daily and meditating on it, then the will of the Father is open to you and within you. You can now boldly come to the throne of God and command that the earth, the situations in your life, and the very thoughts in your mind come in proper alignment with the will of your King.

Finally, the end goal of reading, meditation, and prayer is that they produce yielded and obedient soldiers. Your obedience is the strongest weapon that you have. When one is willingly obedient to God, because of love and fellowship with Him, our obedience serves a crushing blow to the kingdom of darkness, as yet another person willingly rejected its influence. The more people who reject the kingdom of darkness, the more territory it loses, and the more that the Kingdom of God gains. You are only as strong as your obedience to God. You are only as powerful as your activated K-Gene. Consistent reading of Scripture, meditating, praying, and obedience to your King culminate in activated and strengthened K-Genes. These are your weapons, and though they are not all visible, they are mighty and superior to all other forces.

NOTES OF REFLECTION

CONCLUSION

God intentionally crafted you and formed you to win! You have a genetic predisposition for victory, and there is an inheritance with your name on it. God intends for you to live a life of success. However, the mere presence of success means that the chance of failure is lurking nearby. What does this mean for you? It means that victory and success are choices. And it is *your* choice. No one can make you successful, and no one can make you fail. The choice has always been yours, and the pathway to your victory has always been outlined for you. As God's Kingdom is superior to all other entities, true and lasting victory can only be found in Kingdom. That is why God uniquely designed each of us with Kingdom genetics, of the K-Gene.

He knew that we would pursue whatever we desired. He put His K-Gene within us so that we would act like Him, share the same appetite, desires, and pursuits. The key to reactivating His genetic code is through acceptance of Jesus Christ. He was the one anointed by God to reverse the spiritual mutations that humanity suffered due to disobedience and sin. Jesus is the only way, and He is the start of this good life that God designed for us. Once our K-Gene has been reactivated, God uses life's processes to teach us how to simply exist as who we are.

It is impossible to willingly activate the K-Gene and then attempt to hide in the shadows, unnoticed and unbothered. Those outstanding bills, that unruly coworker, that medical diagnosis that you just received, these are all aspects of life that God uses to bring us to the place of *being* who He said we are.

You have learned who you are, and what you are capable of when yielding to God's Kingdom mandate. Victory has always been the end goal in God's mind, and He earnestly wants to win with you on His side. It is time for you to move from potential to manifestation! It is time that you receive your long-overdue inheritance and exercise your authority in the earth. It is time that you matured, to be an adult heir who is capable of birthing systems, shifting environments, and building legacies for God's glory to fill the earth.

Whatever you do, don't give up, don't lose faith. God is greater that any force you can imagine, and because you are made in His image and likeness, you have His weapons to use in the war against the kingdom of darkness! It's time for you to live again! It is time to unlock and activate the K-Gene.

NOTES OF REFLECTION